Wikified Schools

Using Wikis to Improve Collaboration and Communication in Education

Wikified Schools

Using Wikis to Improve Collaboration and Communication in Education

Stephanie D. Sandifer

All Web URLs in this book are correct as of the publication date but may have become inactive or otherwise modified since that time. If you notice a deactivated or changed link, please visit the book wiki: http://wikifiedschools.com for updated information.

For more information:

Wakefield Publishing
506 Willard
Houston, Texas 77006

ISBN 978-0-578-01234-6

For Clare, Austin, and Dillan.
Thank you for enriching my life and
making all of my dreams come true.

Wikified Schools

Table of Contents

Tables, Figures, and Sidebars

Acknowledgments

This book could not have been written without the "critical friendship" of many people. I want to first thank my entire online Personal Learning Network (PLN) which consists of hundreds of people with whom I connect, collaborate, and learn on a daily basis. Through our shared learning and our challenging conversations I gained the knowledge and skill to make this book possible. I am unable to list all of these people here – you know who you are because we connect on our blogs, through Twitter, on one of many wikis or Ning networks, or through Facebook.

I also want to thank my current group of colleagues who have been willing to try this "new thing" called a wiki, and who have challenged me and supported my interest in pushing the envelope in order to improve the quality of our work together. So many of the talented and brave souls in our department have welcomed the opportunity to explore this new way of working and I feel so fortunate to work with such a wonderful group. Tina Angelo and Paula Pierre especially have been so supportive and enthusiastic in exploring the possibilities of using a wiki with our network of teacher-leaders.

I would not be the learning professional that I am today without the friendship and support of my first "team." Christinia Wehde-Roddiger, Maria Aguilar, Patricia Alexander, and Debra Jaques helped me learn through experience what it takes to develop an effective, high performing team, and I will always value the memories of our work together. It shapes my decisions and my actions to this very day.

On a similar note, I also want to thank everyone who has been a part of my learning experience around school improvement. I am especially thankful every day for all of my experiences with the staff of Houston A Plus. Their support and guidance across multiple initiatives has been incredibly valuable to me. I also want to thank Grace Sammon and Cindy Martin for their highly informed support, guidance, and friendship over the past several years.

Finally, and most importantly, I want to thank my family for their love and support. I could not have written this book without your love and your inspiration. Thank you for all that you do and all that you are to me.

Introduction

This book is about change. This book is also about collaboration, creativity, communication, and how to use a powerful web-based technology to achieve all these things much more effectively and efficiently. This book is about technology, but it is also about best practice. How do we leverage technology — specifically wikis and other web-based tools — to improve our collaboration, communication, creative thinking, problem-solving, and change processes? How do we make better use of our time and better use of technology resources such as server space and email? How do we model 21st-Century tools for better communication and collaboration across all levels of our educational organizations?

I know firsthand the difficulties in communication and collaborating in a school environment. I know the challenges all educational leaders face when trying to implement new programs and new initiatives. I know from my experience as a teacher what it feels like to get conflicting or inadequate information from school or district leadership and I understand the urge to resist change by shutting the classroom door. I also understand from personal experience how it feels to work at the district office on collaborative teams that rely extensively on effective communication and collaboration among the members to produce curriculum and instructional products that must be shared with campuses in an effective way that results in improved practice at the campus level. One could say that "I've looked at life from both sides now" and I know that everyone in the system faces many challenges in effective and efficient communication and collaboration. In fact, in my work with school reform I have come to the conclusion that one of our biggest challenges in school improvement at any level is communication (or the lack thereof) followed closely by ineffective collaboration. Prior to my experience with Web 2.0 technologies, I frequently searched for more effective ways of working with my team members and better ways of communicating with individuals as well as with groups of teachers and administrators. As I began exploring the world of Web 2.0 I finally stumbled across tools that made it much easier to achieve my goals and to be much more productive. The most powerful of all of these new tools is the wiki.

I will save the "what are wikis?" discussion for the remainder of the book. Before we begin discussing the what, so what, and now what of wiki use and adoption, let me provide a warning: wikis are not silver bullets. There is no promise made anywhere in this book that wiki adoption will be easy or pain-free in your organization. Faculty and staff are accustomed to many other ways of working — even though those ways may not be as effective or as efficient in achieving the outcomes desired by the organization. You will be moving their cheese. They will resist. You and everyone else involved in moving forward with wiki adoption must remain persistent in your efforts. No change is ever easy and the "status quo" can be a stubborn opponent. The success of wiki adoption in your organization will depend heavily on the leadership at all levels within your organization. Technology alone does not create a utopia.

Finally and most importantly, this book is about learning. As educators — as "learning professionals" — our work is learning. We are tasked with facilitating the learning of others, but also of facilitating our own learning. It is my firm belief that everything that is done in a school and within a school district should be focused on what is best for the students and not what is easiest or most comfortable for the adults. The use of a wiki should result in better use of time, improved communication, and increased adult learning, which should contribute to improved student learning. Ward Cunningham, the developer of the very first wiki software, once described the wiki as “The simplest thing that could possibly work” (Venners, 2004). Needless to say however, the initial use of a wiki will not be comfortable or easy for adults who are not familiar with it. It is easy to avoid changing practice when “the old way” is more comfortable, even if “the old way” is less efficient and less effective. Educators want to be viewed as skilled professionals and are more likely to prefer being competent at the old wrong thing than incompetent at the new right thing (Black and Gregersen, 2002). In order to improve student learning, we must be model learners. We must be lead learners. So step out of your comfort zone and join me as we explore the use of wikis in our work.

Chapter 1: Organization and Collaboration in the B.W. (Before Wiki) Era

"To succeed in this new world, it will not be enough — indeed, it will be counterproductive — simply to intensify current policies, management strategies, and curricular approaches." — Tapscott and Williams

Ask any educator what his or her "core mission" is and most will respond with something along the lines of "education" or "learning" or "success for all students." Most of our schools and our school districts include this language in their mission statements. Ask any educator what his or her number one priority is in daily responsibilities, the response will usually relate to this mission of "education for all." This is a noble mission to undertake, and many educators find it to be a most challenging task. The business of educating learners has become more complex over the past century and our school systems have responded by adding more layers of everything from curriculum standards and policies, management and bureaucracy, to school structures and state and federal laws. The traditional approach to managing all these elements has been a hierarchical structure rooted in early 20th-Century management theory pioneered by German sociologist Max Weber (Lunenburg and Ornstein, 2004), and with little variation, this model has dominated educational system structure throughout the past century.

In the late 20th-Century, management theory began to

focus more on collaboration and flat organizations and less on hierarchical methods of organization. The education field gradually began to adopt the language of this movement towards building "learning organizations" (Senge et. al., 2000). While educational leaders speak the language and promote more collaborative cultures in their "learning organizations," the primary means of organization remains rooted in a hierarchical structure where decisions are made at the top and are handed down to the lower levels through mandates with very little input from the faculty and staff assigned to the campuses. The decision-making process is quite often very lengthy requiring multiple stages of review, revision, and approval from multiple supervisors. In larger districts, information and communications between and among departments and campuses is complicated if not nonexistent.

In the book *Here Comes Everybody*, Clay Shirky explains the difficulties faced by traditional hierarchical organizations as they strive to achieve their "core missions":

> "Running an organization is difficult in and of itself, no matter what its goals. Every transaction it undertakes — every contract, every agreement, every meeting — requires it to expend some limited resource: time, attention, or money. Because of these transaction costs, some sources of value are too costly to take advantage of. As a result, no institution can put all its energies into pursuing its mission; it must expend considerable effort on maintaining discipline and structure, simply to keep itself viable. Self-preservation of the institution becomes job number one, while its stated goal is relegated to number two or lower, no matter what the mission statement says." (Shirky, 2008)

The key statement in the passage quoted above is where Shirky writes that "its stated goal is relegated to number two or lower, no matter what the mission statement says." What happens in our schools if our stated goal of improving student learning is relegated to number two status because the efforts to maintain discipline and structure pull our resources of time, attention, and money away from the focus on learning? Can you think of specific instances where other issues took precedence over a focus on learning on your campus?

Now look at your typical contemporary school district. Visit your local school district's website and take the following test:

- Locate a list of district departments. How many are there?
- Locate curriculum documents.
- Locate information about athletic facilities.
- Find a staff directory.
- Locate the technology equipment standards.
- Locate the weekly lunch menu.
- Locate purchasing procedures.
- Locate up-to-date employee memos.
- View the current district calendar and make note of how many district-level meetings are listed. Are they listed?

Note how long it took and how many levels of web pages were needed to find information. Are any of the documents located behind password-protected portals? Why?

Here is another exercise. Stop what you are doing right now and look around your office. How many three-ring binders do you see? How many bookshelves are taken up with those binders? When was the last time you opened one of those binders? How useful is this printed information if you never refer to it, and how much waste occurs from the excessive printing of documents that simply sit on office and classroom shelves after the training, in-service, or meeting has ended?

The point of these exercises is to build awareness of the complexity of a typical district organization. This complexity mirrors what Shirky describes above, and it begs the question: How good are we at staying focused on our number one priority of "educating all students"? If you have spent even one semester in an educational leadership position, you have enough experience to know the demands placed upon everyone in the system, and the difficulty in focusing on the mission when faced with numerous meetings, action items, the barrage of emails, endless and often redundant paperwork requirements, and the always unpredictable "emergency."

Conscientious education leaders should ask themselves: Isn't there a better way to manage all this information and communication? There is and we call it a “wiki.”

Chapter 2: What is a wiki?

You might be surprised to learn that wikis are older than the recent Web 2.0 technologies that are so prevalent across the Internet. Wikis have been around since the mid-1990's when the first wiki, the WikiWikiWeb, was developed by Ward Cunningham. The word "wiki" is the Hawaiian word for "fast," and as you become more familiar with how wikis work you will see why that term is so appropriate. Wikipedia, which is perhaps the most commonly known wiki, includes the following definition on the entry for "wiki":

> "A wiki is software that allows users to create, edit, and link pages together with ease. Wikis are often used to create collaborative websites and to power community websites. These wiki websites are often also referred to as wikis; for example, Wikipedia is one of the best-known wikis. Wikis are used in many businesses to provide affordable and effective Intranets and for Knowledge Management."

Essentially, a wiki is a website that can be edited by anyone or by anyone with appropriate privileges if the wiki is restricted to registered users. Most importantly, a wiki is a website that can be edited by anyone without needing to know

HTML or some other scripting language. At the most basic level, wikis can be edited as easily as editing a document in a word processor or writing an email. While wikis are simple to use, they can include added functionality that give the users a robust set of collaborative features including embedded media such as videos, streaming video, slideshows, shared calendars, databases, and RSS feeds, to name a few.

Despite the common misperception (due to media coverage of Wikipedia) that wikis are open documents that are vulnerable to vandalism, wikis can be tightly secured with access restricted to employees and staff and sections of wikis can be more open to the public to allow collaboration between the school and home. We need to distinguish between a public wiki such as Wikipedia, and enterprise wikis that companies worldwide are adopting within their organizations. Wikipedia is an example of the use of crowdsourcing (Howe, 2006) on a large and public scale, whereas enterprise wikis typically tend to be a method for intra-organization knowledge management, project management, collaboration, meeting management, and communication.

Enterprise wikis still rely on the "wisdom of the crowd" to develop knowledge and products in a collaborative space. The biggest differences are access, control, and number of participants. Enterprise wikis also provide functionality that allows pieces of content to be grouped together in what is usually referred to as "spaces." The spaces can be set up according to department, school, team, or project, and access to each space can be limited to specific users. Typically, enterprise wikis are not open to the public and access to the wiki can be tightly control by wiki administrators. One enterprise wiki can contain open spaces and closed spaces with access open or limited to all those spaces based on the school or organization preferences. Security on the enterprise wiki can allow read and write access, read-only access, or no access. High-end enterprise wikis also allow integration with other systems such as school or district email. As we will see in later chapters, even the free wiki hosting services offer many of these features and provide very effective security for education-related wikis allowing schools and districts a free alternative for learning about and getting started with wiki use in the organization.

Chapter 3: Why use a wiki?

A few of the many companies that are embracing wiki use in their organizations include: Boeing, Best Buy/Geek Squad, BMW, Xerox, IBM, Disney, DHL, Proctor & Gamble, Thompson Learning, Ford Motor Company, Texas Instruments. These and other companies are finding that the use of wikis for communication, collaboration and knowledge management has a positive impact on productivity, lowers production costs, increases creativity and innovation, and improves overall team collaboration. This becomes increasingly critical as companies expand globally with dispersed teams working in different time zones, different countries, and entirely different continents. In the book, *Wikinomics: How Mass Collaboration Changes Everything*, authors Don Tapscott and Anthony Williams predict that "as a growing number of firms see the benefits of mass collaboration, this new way of organizing will eventually displace the traditional corporate structures as the company's primary engine of wealth creation" (Tapscott and Williams, 2007).

As we shall see in examples throughout this book, the culture that emerges from the use of a wiki is more in alignment with Rensis Likert's System 4 Organization (see Table 3.1) where subordinate ideas are solicited and used by administrators, communication flows freely in all directions, decisions are decentralized and made throughout the organization at all levels, and goals are set by group participation (Likert, 1967). Of course, this also requires leadership grounded in Theory Y which assumes that educators are professionals who accept and seek responsibility (McGregor, 1960). Wiki adoption will not thrive under heavily bureaucratic structures that rely on directives and control.

Table 3.1: Comparison of System 1 and System 4 Organization

Organizational Characteristics	System 1 Organization	System 2 Organization
Leadership	Little confidence and trust between administrators and subordinates	Subordinate ideas are solicited and used by administrators
Motivation	Taps fear, status, and economic motives exclusively	Taps all major motives except fear
Communication	One-way, downward communication	Communication flows freely in all directions
Interaction-influence	Little upward influence; downward influence overestimated	Substantial influence upward, downward, and horizontally
Decision making	Centralized; decisions made at the top	Decentralized; decision made throughout the organization
Goal setting	Established by top-level administrators and communicated downward	Established by group participation
Control	Close over-the-shoulder supervision	Emphasis on self-control
Performance goals	Low and passively sought by administrators; little commitment to developing human resources	High and actively sought by administrators; full commitment to developing human resources

Likert, R. (1967). *The Human Organization*. New York: McGraw-Hill.

In his book *Wikipatterns: A practical guide to improving productivity and collaboration in your organization*, Stewart Mader explains why wikis are growing in use across organizations in a variety of industries:

> "The wiki is rapidly growing in name recognition and use in organizations because its simple design and function enables equal participation by people at all

levels of technology knowledge and savvy. On top of that, it has an unprecedented ability to adapt to different uses, bring people together and strengthen teams, and promote a collaborative approach to problems." (Mader, 2008)

The value in that for educational organizations, districts, and schools is that the technology is appropriate for novice users, which allows for an easy-to-use collaborative environment that can increase knowledge and cooperation across the entire organization. Additionally, because the wiki can be edited by anyone, it enables the "flattening" of the organization which generates more ownership of initiatives where everyone can contribute to the collective knowledge base as well as the planning and implementation of new initiatives. The wiki truly creates a "paradigm shift" in terms of organization and participation — bringing the organization closer to Level 4 Organization (Table 3.1) than current models. This is crucial in education organizations that have been striving to become "learning organizations" (Senge et. al., 2000), but have yet to move away from hierarchical bureaucratic structures.

In addition to the organizational changes that are enabled by the use of wikis, electronic storage and email management are relieved by the reduction in "attachments" emailed across the organization. This will make email servers as well as employees much happier! The information and communication flow is clearly expressed in Figure 3.1, a graphic that was created by Chris Rassmussen for use in training at the U.S. National Geospatial Intelligence Agency.

The European investment bank Dresdner Kleinwort Wasserstein is one example of the impact of wiki use on organization resources. Wiki use which originated through an informal, grass-roots process in their IT department has now spread across the company and has resulted in a 75 percent drop in email volume and a 50 percent cut in meeting time which in turn has resulted in greater productivity and more effective organization-wide collaboration (Tapscott and Williams, 2007). Imagine that kind of reduction in email volume and meeting time in your school or district offices. How much more time would become available to your staff that they could use to focus on instruction and student learning? How many more productive hours could your staff find in their current weekly schedules?

Figure 3.1 – Email vs. Wiki Collaboration

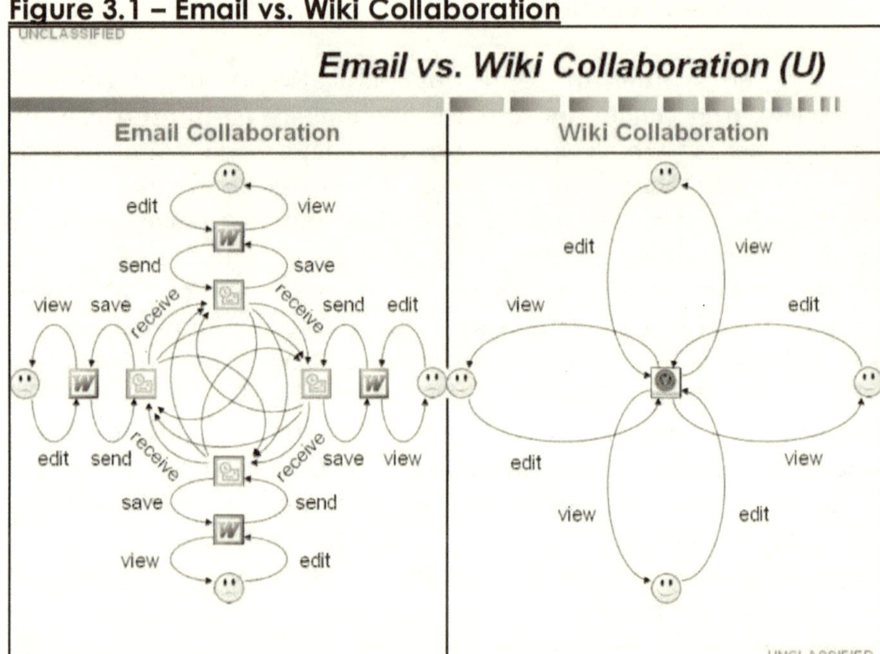

Source: Chris Rasmussen at US National Geospatial Intelligence Agency via http://www.wikinomics.com/blog/index.php/2008/03/29/wiki-collaboration-leads-to-happiness-updated-and-revisited/

Let's explore a few examples of how your organization can be changed through the adoption of wikis:

Scenario: Principal Jones wants to see what other campuses are doing for student interventions.

Before Wiki - B.W.

He emails a few other principals who are friends of his on Monday morning. By that afternoon one of the other principals emails him back with a Word document. The next day two other principals email him back with brief explanations in the emails and another principal forwards the request to his Dean of Instruction to fulfill. By the end of the week he still hasn't heard from one of the principals. Figure 3.2 provides an example of how documents are currently scattered around the various campuses.

Figure 3.2 – Before Wiki Document Collections

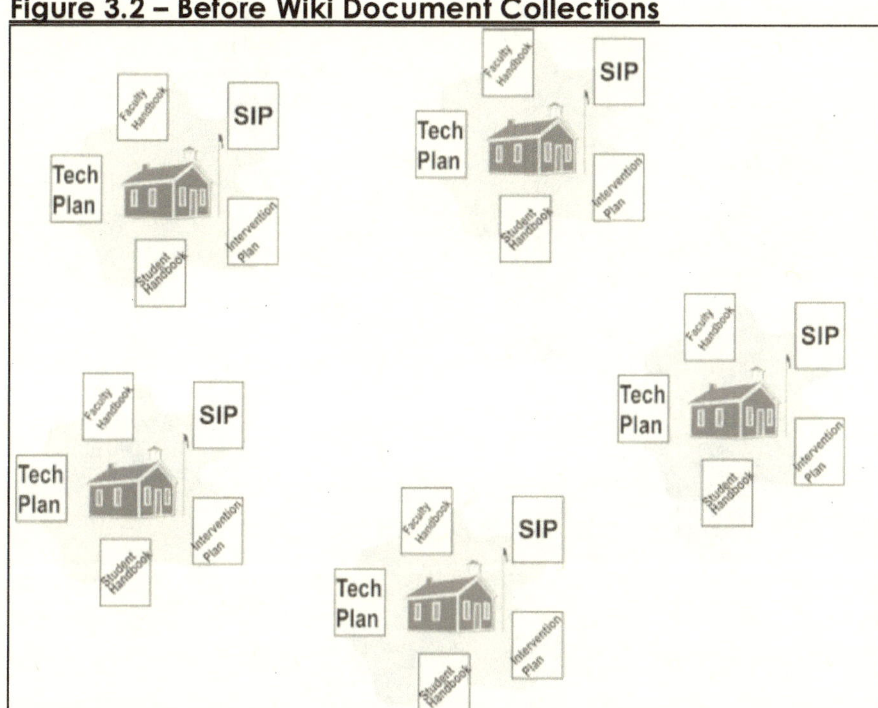

Before Wiki (B.W.) All documents are scattered across campuses and are not easily accessible to personnel on different campuses.

After Wiki - A.W.

He searches on the word "interventions" in the district-wide wiki and within seconds has a list of all the intervention plans for every school in the district. The intervention plans, which are contained on their own pages within the wiki are complete and up-to-date and provide Principal Jones with a complete picture of what is happening on other campuses in his district. Figure 3.3 provides an example of how documents and plans can be centrally located within a district-wide wiki.

Scenario: A team from Central High School attends a national education conference — paid for with school funds

— with the expectation that they will bring back what they learn to the campus to share with other teachers.

Figure 3.3 – After Wiki Document Collections

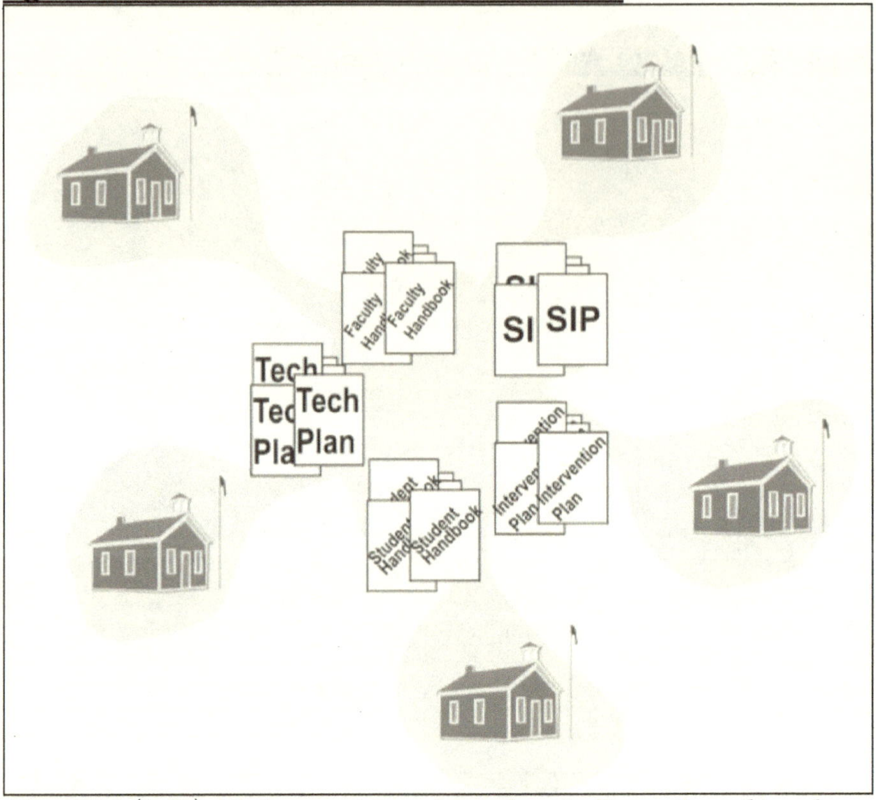

After Wiki (A.W.) All documents are located centrally on the wiki and are easily accessible to personnel on different campuses.

Before Wiki - B.W.

Individual members of the team take notes in a variety of ways: one uses a laptop, two others use a notebook or a journal, and the last two just take notes on the back of handouts that they get at each session they attend. The team gets together on the last night at the conference to compare notes and discuss ideas for professional development sessions they can facilitate when they get back. Two months later they meet again to plan the professional development — some of the team members bring their notes to the meeting and some forget to bring their notes.

After Wiki - A.W.

The team creates a conference wiki where each of them takes their notes live while sitting in individual sessions. One page of the wiki is set up to build the professional development agenda that they will use when they return to campus. They list professional development session proposals on the page so the team can vote on the most relevant sessions to offer when they return. They meet briefly upon their return to campus to discuss logistics then they share the complete agenda with the principal for approval. Two months later they deliver the professional development and share the entire wiki (including all their notes) with the entire faculty. (A lengthier, more detailed description of this is highlighted in Chapter 4)

Scenario: The district's Director of Curriculum wants to create an ad hoc committee to develop a curriculum for "digital citizenship and 21st-Century literacy"

Before Wiki - B.W.

The director posts an announcement on the district-wide intranet then spends the next two months interviewing interested candidates as they stumble upon the announcement and submit their letters of interest. After two months the committee is seated, and they spend the next four months meeting once every two weeks for two hours after school. They eventually provide the director with a proposed curriculum presented in a three-ring binder.

After Wiki - A.W.

The director performs a search in the wiki on the terms "digital citizenship" and "21st-Century literacy." The results include links to staff profiles and portfolios that include those phrases. The director sifts through the profiles to locate staff members who have been involved in related projects then reviews their wiki activity to see who is most active in collaborating on a variety of projects. From the list, the director invites a selected group of staff members to interview for the committee. The interviews take less than two days. The committee meets in person once every two weeks for two hours after school while also collaborating on a regular basis through the wiki. After one month they contact the director and ask her to review the proposed curriculum that they have developed on the wiki. The director approves the curriculum and the wiki pages of the proposed curriculum are moved to the district's online curriculum wiki.

Scenario: A committee from Central Middle School needs to develop a five-day professional development schedule for August when the teachers return from summer break.

Before Wiki - B.W.

The committee members spend the first few weeks emailing resources to each other with ideas for various kinds of professional development they can include during that August week. They schedule a meeting, but a couple of the committee members can't attend the meeting because of family commitments. The members who can meet come together without an agenda to just brainstorm and discuss some of the ideas that were emailed. The meeting ends with no firm decisions and the team decides to meet again the following week. At the next meeting they are able to decide on some of the ideas, and they begin plugging ideas into the five-day schedule. They have three more meetings over the next month to finalize the schedule. A couple of the suggested sessions require contracts with external service providers and two committee members communicate with the service providers to arrange the dates and times of their sessions. Plans are still not completely finalized by the end of the school year and the committee has to meet two more times during the summer to finalize the plans.

After Wiki - A.W.

The committee has an initial organizing meeting to discuss a plan of action using the wiki. They create a wiki page just for planning and spend the next two weeks contributing ideas, voting on ideas and plugging ideas into the wiki. After three weeks they meet again to review the current plan then one of them emails the principal asking her to review the plan as it is on the wiki for approval. The principal suggests a few revisions on the discussion section of the planning page and a couple of committee members make the suggested changes. After the principal approves the plan, the committee uses the wiki to develop agendas, handouts, and presentations for the sessions that they have each volunteered to facilitate. Wiki pages are shared with a couple of external service providers who have been contracted to come in to provide professional development on a couple of specific topics. By the end of the school year the committee has finalized the plans. During the summer, the committee easily adjusts the plans as needed through the wiki with no need for any in-person meetings.

Scenario: The Data Team from Central Middle School needs to create a Data Inventory to have a summary of all internal and external assessments used in the school (Boudett, City, and Murnane, 2005)

Before Wiki - B.W.

The Data Team creates a table in a Word document then emails it out to the entire faculty for input. By the end of one week the Data Team has received replies from only eight staff members. One member of the Data Team takes all the replies that contain edited versions of the Word document and spends time copying and pasting all the edits from the individual documents into one document. The Data Team sends out the document again to get more responses. After three weeks the Data Team shares the entire inventory with the Leadership Team at their monthly meeting and find out from some members of the Leadership Team that some assessments are missing from the inventory.

After Wiki - A.W.

The Data Team creates a table on one page of the campus wiki and sends an email to the entire faculty with a link to the wiki page. They give the faculty a deadline of two weeks to input information they have on the various assessments used on campus. The Data Team emails the Leadership Team with a link to the wiki page so that the Leadership Team can monitor the development of the inventory then discuss the results at their next meeting. At the next Leadership Team meeting, one member of the Data Team opens the wiki page on their laptop and fills in any missing information to complete the inventory at that time.

As you can see from these examples, there are many situations where wikis can be used to improve processes as well as individual and team productivity. With the exceptions of confidential student and employee information, most information within any school or district can be shared more effectively and more efficiently through the systemic use of an enterprise wiki. As with any change in practice, implementation of an enterprise wiki is not without challenges, and it will require persistence on the part of leaders. However, as with any effective change process, the most effective approach incorporates both a top-down and a grassroots, bottom-up implementation. District or school leaders should set the groundwork by supporting the implementation and making the necessary changes within the system to ensure organization-wide adoption while also locating and enlisting the assistance of "early adopters" at lower levels of the organization. These "early adopters" can be more effective in spreading adoption through viral, grassroots methods.

In addition to the productivity benefits for the adults, the use of a wiki increases adult competency with the technology that is being used in the workplace that our students will enter when they complete their education. This allows us to understand and own the technology, which enables us to be more effective in helping students learn how to use these tools productively. These are the "workplace skills" that we need to be teaching and we need to know how to use them in our own work as well. Will Richardson, an edublogger and author of *Blogs, Wikis, & Podcasts in the Classroom*, states that teachers have to be "colearners" who model their own use of these tools and must understand "the practical pedagogical implications of these technologies" in order to be effective in preparing students for a highly-networked and global future (Richardson, 2008).

In the chapter "How: Making it work in your organization" we will explore the nuts and bolts of implementing the adoption of wiki use across your organization. First, let's explore some more specific examples of how wikis can be used across our schools and our districts.

Reflection Questions

How does the information in this chapter change your thinking around the use of technology in professional activities?
What questions does this information raise for you?
How might this information influence your work as an educator?

Chapter 4: When & Where

As we have seen, the versatility of a wiki allows for a variety of uses within an educational organization. Wikis can be useful for district office departments, intradistrict teams, school administration and leadership teams, campus department or grade level teams, and in a variety of other settings. In fact, wiki use can be unlimited with regard to non-sensitive information, however, no one should store student or employee personal information on a wiki. Even with that limitation, the impact of wiki use in a school or district office can dramatically improve nearly all operational processes.

Wikis for Leadership and Administration

School leadership is complex and demanding. Very few school administrators are successful in their leadership without good organization skills, effective time management strategies, and effective communication skills. Even with these skills, many school administrators struggle with competing demands for their time, crisis management, and an always over-flowing "in box." The skilled and effective implementation of wiki use by a campus leader can be critical for anyone seeking a way to work smarter and not harder. As we shall learn, wikis provide educational leaders with an easy-to-use tool for archiving work, managing documentation and information, and more effective and efficient team collaboration.

The following chart aligns educational processes and practices with corporate practices that are frequently managed or facilitated through the use of a wiki.

Business	**Schools and Districts**
Collaborative Intelligence	Professional Learning Communities
Documentation	Memos, policies and procedures, forms, and other documents
Participatory Collective Knowledge Base	Professional Learning Communities Critical Friends Groups
Project Management	Grant Writing and Grant Program Management
Tacit Knowledge	Collection of Veteran Teachers' knowledge about instruction, classroom management, and pedagogy
Meeting Management	Meeting Agenda Development Meeting Minutes/Notes Meeting Archives
Encyclopedia	Curriculum and Instruction Clearing House/Knowledge Base
Business Social Networks	Professional Learning Networks, Personal Learning Networks
Flexible Client Collaboration	School/Home Collaboration Collaboration with Business Partners

While many of the uses listed above relate to collaborative team planning and documentation, wikis can also be used by individuals as a personal online "notebook" where information can be documented, organized, and archived. Resources can be uploaded or linked to within the wiki, and all content can be easily transferred to other documents or other wikis depending on the need. This is one of the best ways to explore and learn about the use of wiki as it provides a private space for experimentation.

Communication and Knowledge Management

In *Change Leadership,* Tony Wagner outlines Seven Disciplines for Strengthening Instruction, and one of these disciplines is "Meetings About the Work." In his explanation, he criticizes the typical staff meetings that are concerned only with announcements and operations rather than the work of effective instruction. He explains that the usual agenda items would be better left to memos (and by implication — emails) in order to leave the meeting time for professional development around effective instruction or reflection on current instructional practices (Wagner, Kegan, and et al, 2006).

Douglas Reeves also addresses what he refers to as "pointless meetings" in his book *The Learning Leader* (2006) when he states that "Appreciation, recognition, and personal contact are some of the most extraordinarily strategic uses of leadership time, yet time is rarely allocated in that way because we are too busy with expenditures of time that are distinguished only by tradition and expectation, not by effectiveness." By this he means that too often we insist on holding the typical monthly staff meetings or weekly team meetings out of habit, and that these habits result in wasted time. Both Reeves and Wagner suggest that we rethink how we spend our face-to-face time and that we save the announcements and "information sharing" for written memos.

A school or district could use a wiki for sharing announcements and operational information with staff members rather than using memos in .PDF format, emails, or printed memos as Wagner specifically suggests. This would reduce paperwork and save precious storage memory in email accounts and on employee hard drives because the wiki is stored on a server, multiple copies are unnecessary, and all changes are archived on a server. Additionally, the wiki also allows leaders to plan and facilitate team meetings more effectively and efficiently from the planning stage through the follow-up stage. Meeting participants have access to all documentation at all times from all locations, and when face-to-face interaction is not necessary, all participants can collaborate at their individual availability which reduces the stress of trying to coordinate with everyone's personal schedules.

In the 2008-2009 school year, the Curriculum, Instruction, and Assessment Division in the Houston Independent School District (Houston, Texas) began using wikis for collaboration among some of the division's curriculum teams. The first team to implement the use of wiki was the Adolescent Literacy team. Initiated by the two members of the team, the wiki is being successfully implemented within the entire Literacy Support Network that spans across all the middle schools and high schools within the district. The various uses include: Meeting agendas, notes, and feedback; storage of literacy related materials; hosting of slideshows, videos, and other professional learning materials; embedded feedback forms; hosting of photos and other artifacts of the collaborative work; pages for collaborative development of resources and documents (the team also uses Google Docs for collaborative writing and development of agendas, presentations, and documents); and a variety of other resources that contribute to the wiki becoming a "live" and collaboratively developed "Literacy Coach Handbook."

The Literacy Support Network Wiki has become a model for other teams. During the Fall semester the English Language Arts team and the A2TeaMS (Academy of Accomplished Teaching in Math and Science) team started their own wikis to use with the campus-based teacher leaders with whom they each work. By mid-year the Educational Technology team introduced a division-wide wiki for knowledge management across all the curriculum teams within the division. The division is becoming "wikified" and many team members are beginning to understand the benefits provided by the use of wikis for all of the division's work.

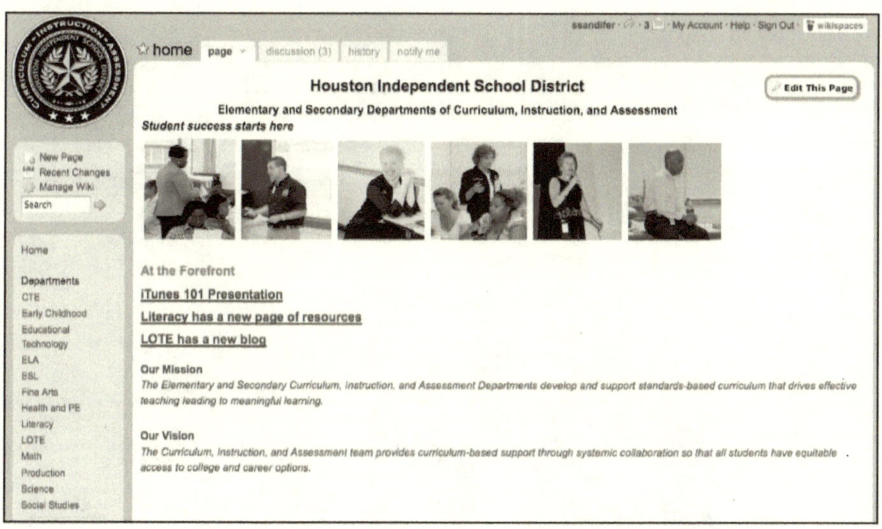

The Houston Independent School District's Elementary and Secondary Departments of Curriculum, Instruction, and Assessment have developed a wiki for interdepartmental knowledge management and resource sharing. Launched in the Fall of 2008, the new wiki is not only a space for collaboration and communication, it is also a place for the team members to learn and model 21st-Century skills.

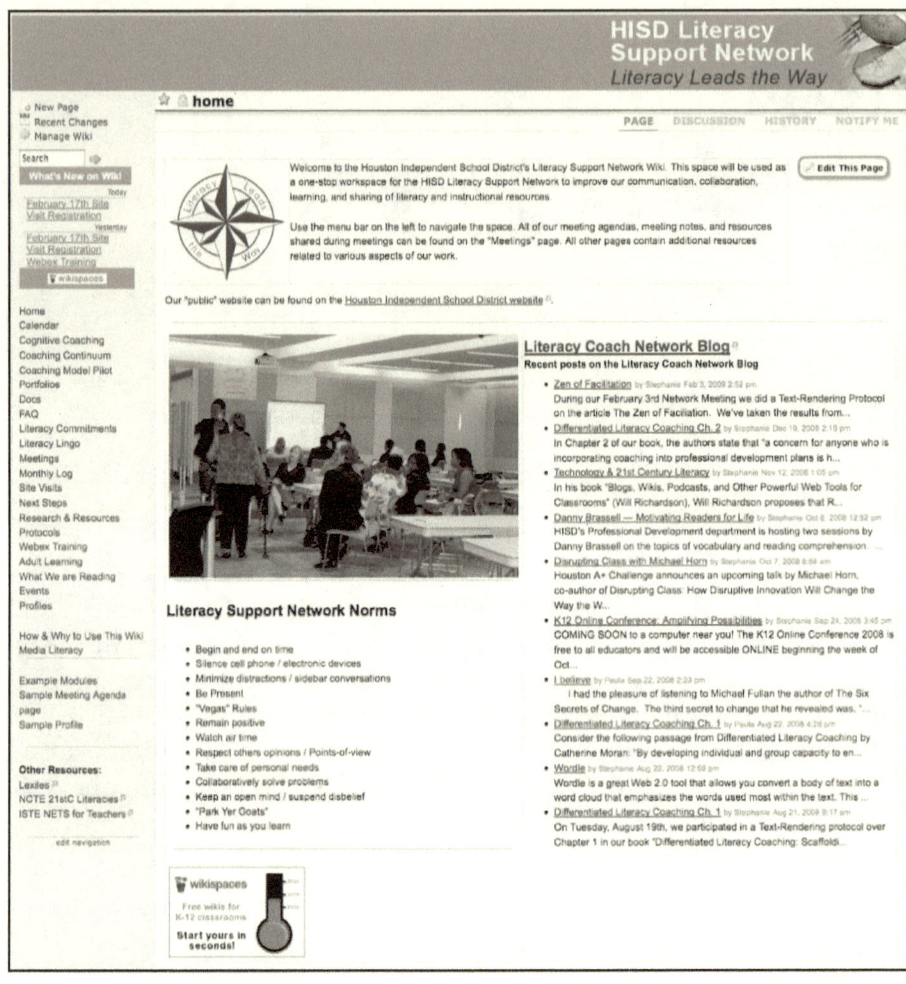

The Literacy Support Network's wiki provides a one-stop "shop" for all of the materials and resources required by the members of the network. A separate blog is also incorporated by embedding the blog's RSS feed.

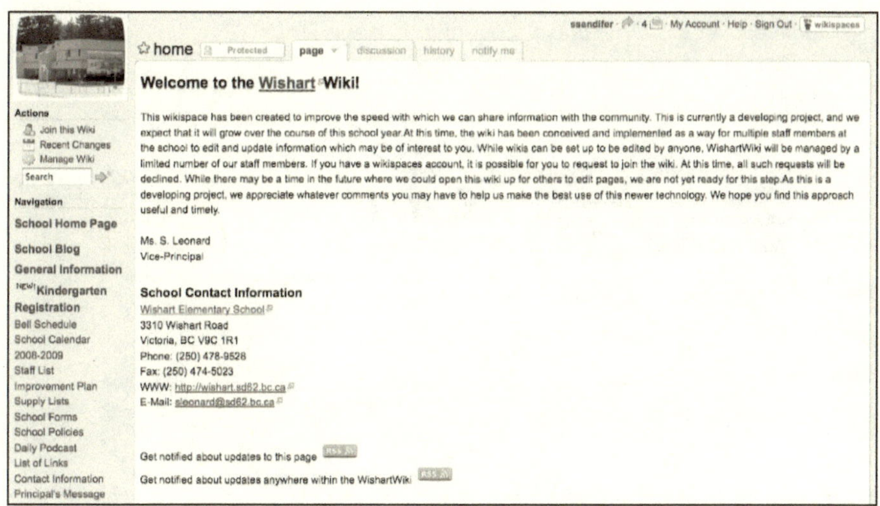

Wishart Elementary School in British Columbia uses a wiki for everything from publishing information to the community to publishing internal policies and documents for faculty and students.

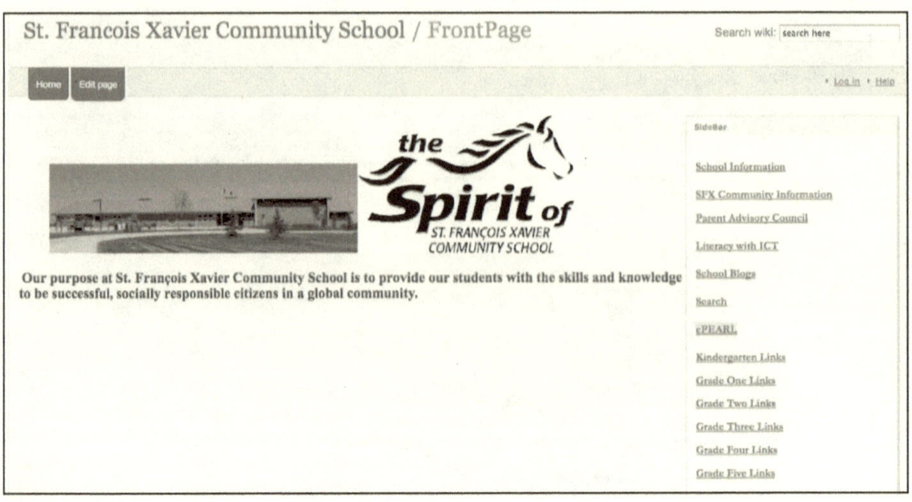

St. Francis Xavier School and St. Laurent School in Winnipeg have created school wikis for communicating with faculty, staff, parents, and the general public. Both wikis include resources for teachers as well as general information that is helpful to parents and students.

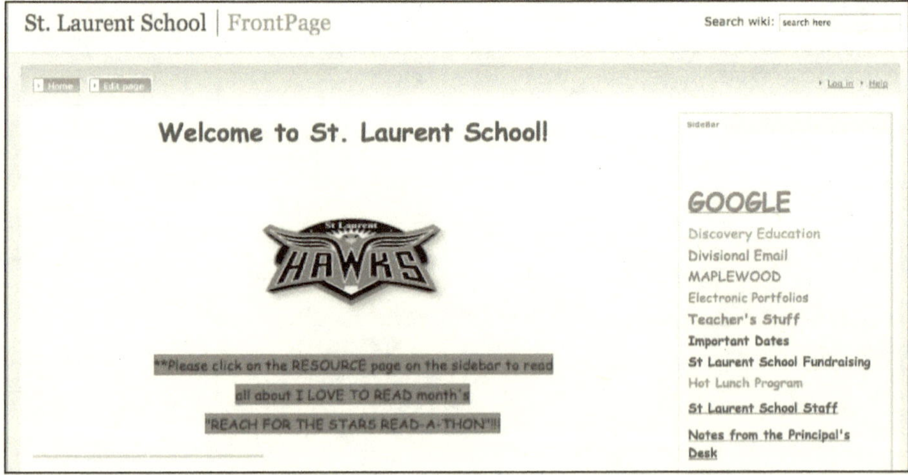

School Improvement Plans, Technology Plans, and more...

Wikis can be used to build and maintain action plans including but not limited to: School Improvement Plans, Technology Plans, Grant Proposals, Departmental Action Plans, and Special Project Plans.

Perhaps the most valuable of these is the use of a wiki for developing and maintaining a School Improvement Plan. In fact, a wiki as the School Improvement Plan could be the most collaborative, truly "living" document that drives school improvement on a daily basis. Rather than just working from multiple copies of (at best) an electronic text document, the framework for the School Improvement Plan could be copied into a wiki and team members could make their edits directly into the wiki. This is one of those uses that work very well for freeing up email memory space. School Improvement Plan documents can grow to become quite large and if trying to collaborate via email with several team members they can quickly clog up multiple email inboxes as one copy becomes many copies across the team. Considerations would have to be made with regard to structure, and it might be helpful to also make use of Google Docs for the initial drafting of the School Improvement Plan.

If you have ever worked on a grant proposal you are aware of the complexity of the task. The best proposals are usually drafted by a school team, and once again, as we have seen in the previous examples, a wiki (with or without the addition of Google Docs) is an excellent way to manage the collaborative writing process. Each section of the grant proposal can have its own wiki page and specific references of the research supporting the proposal can easily be linked to the original sources if they are online. If a district has a district-wide wiki, the grant management department could create wiki templates for the grant proposals and give each school its own space in which to draft their proposal. This makes the process faster and easier for everyone involved, while streamlining the process from beginning to end.

Wishart School Plan: Goal 1

Goal Area:
Language Arts - Reading

Objective:
To improve students' ability to comprehend what they read

Target:

1. By the Spring of 2009, 90% of our Grade 3 students will read with fluency and comprehension at developmentally appropriate levels. This means that 90% of our general population Grade 3 students will meet or exceed expectations in fluency and comprehension.
2. By the Spring of 2009, 90% of our Grade 6 students will read with fluency and comprehension at developmentally appropriate levels. This means that 90% of our general population Grade 6 students will meet or exceed expectations in fluency and comprehension.
3. By Spring of 2009, 80% of our Grade 4 students will meet/exceed or exceed expectations in reading comprehension on the provincial FSA in Grade 4.

Comprehension Results on the DART - Spring 2005 to Targets in Spring 2009

Grade	2004/05 Meets/Exceeds (Actual) - Before Reading Comprehension Focus	2005/06 Meet/Exceeds (Actual) - Year 1 Reading Comprehension Focus	2006/07 Meets/Exceeds (Actual) - Year 2 Reading Comprehension Focus	2007/08 Meets Exceeds (Target)	2008/09 Meets/Exceeds (Target)
3	15%	54%	70%	80%	90%
4	33%	39%	47%	63%	80%
5	22%	19%	70%	80%	85%
6	28%	33%	75%	83%	90%

Note: A two-year goal of 80% in Grade 4 (compared with a 90% goal for Grade 3) results from an analysis of cohort data. This suggests that as students transition from the primary to the intermediate grades, there is a drop in their achievement as reflected on the DART.

Rationale:
Over the past two years, the school has focused its efforts on the improvement of reading comprehension (as measured on the DRA, DART, and FSA). These efforts have yielded results, as evidenced by the growth between 2004/2005 (before the focus on comprehension) 2005/2006 (the first year of the focus) and

The Wishart Elementary School wiki includes the campus' school improvement plan. This provides the entire school community with easy access to the document.

Transform Meetings

One of the most powerful uses for a wiki across a school or district is the ability to transform the nature, structure, and function of all meetings. As mentioned previously, meetings can be one of the biggest drains on our scarce resource of time. How meetings are planned, structured, and facilitated can make a huge difference in productivity and outcomes within every education organization. The use of a wiki can provide a means of improving many of the processes around meeting development, structure, and facilitation. Of course, a wiki is not a solution for poor facilitation, but those skills can be learned elsewhere and will be greatly enhanced by the use of a wiki.

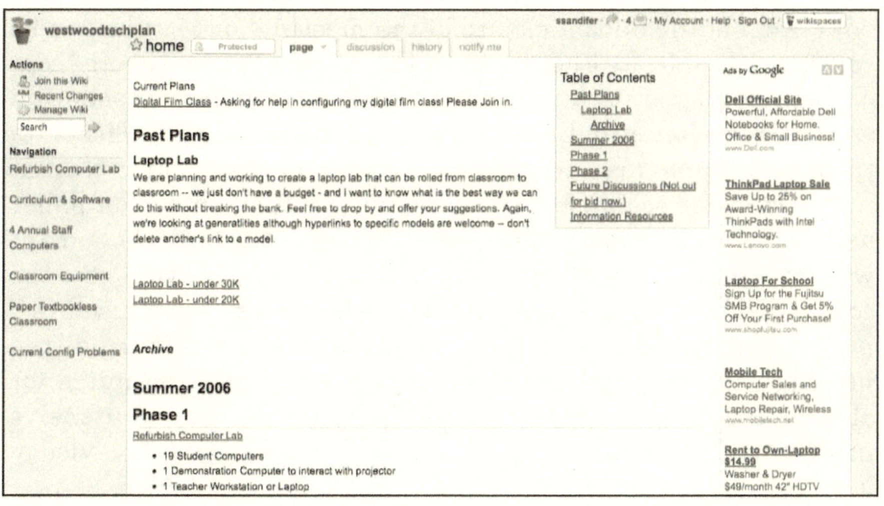

Westwood Technology Plan Wiki is an excellent example of a wiki used for developing and maintaining one school's technology plan. The goals, objectives, planned actions, and needed resources are all accessible to the entire school staff, students, and the community, and the school also uses the wiki to archive older technology plans which is useful when conducing evaluations of programs and initiatives.

We will begin by looking at how we can transform meeting agenda development. Traditionally the meeting organizer sets the agenda for a meeting. At best skilled facilitators who conscientiously plan productive meetings that add value for all participants create these agendas. At worst these agendas are simply laundry lists of information items that are better communicated via email or memo. In the very best scenarios the skilled facilitator generates a skeleton agenda and shares it with participants in advance of the meeting to solicit additional items that need to be placed on the agenda. A wiki can be an ideal place for collaborative meeting agenda development. All participants and stakeholders can access the wiki page and add their own agenda items prior to the meeting. The facilitator can review the proposed agenda items and rearrange the order, time, and resources needed.

During the meeting, notes can be taken directly in the wiki. Depending on the nature of the meeting, one scribe can be selected to generate the notes on the same page as the agenda, or each participant can take his or her own notes on separate wiki pages that are linked from the agenda page. Either of these solutions are acceptable and a marked improvement upon the older scenario where one person takes notes on paper and later transcribes those notes to an electronic document which is emailed out to the participants. Can you see the conservation of time that occurs when wikis are used for meeting notes? Depending on the nature and structure of the meeting, this method can save anywhere from 30 minutes for shorter meetings to a few hours for lengthier more intensive meetings that require debate, brainstorming, and knowledge development.

So what happens after the meeting? In most cases, with the use of a wiki there is little or nothing that is required of the facilitator after the meeting. All participants have access to the wiki and all meeting documentation has already been added to the wiki either before or during the meeting. In some cases the facilitator may want to get feedback from the participants, which can be accomplished by creating a feedback form in Google Docs and embedding the form into the meeting wiki page. In other cases some of the meeting information may need to be crossed-referenced with other information located elsewhere in the larger wiki, and this is easily accomplished by creating hyper-links to those items.

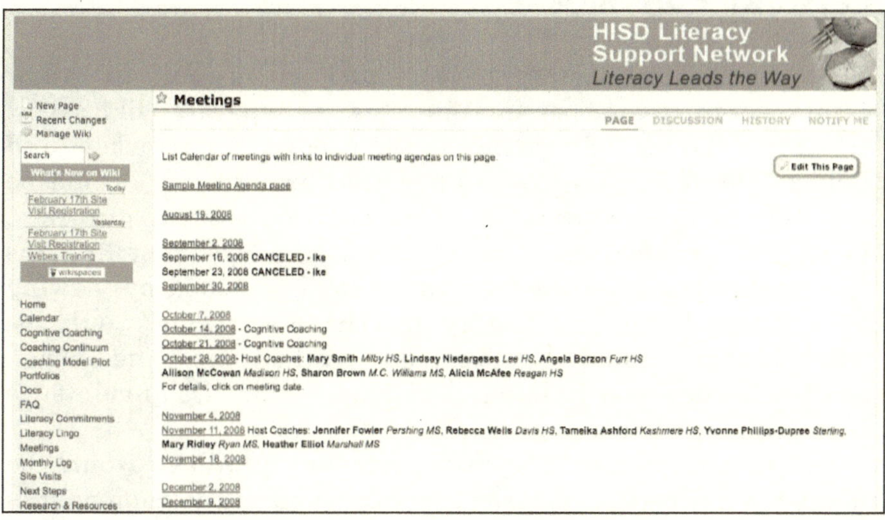

The Literacy Support Network uses its wiki for everything described on the previous pages. You can see in the screenshot above how a "meetings" page is structured and in the following image you can see what one of the meeting pages looks like after a meeting. Notice that the page for the meeting includes the facilitator's agenda, an embedded slideshow, an embedded form for reflections, and the meeting notes.

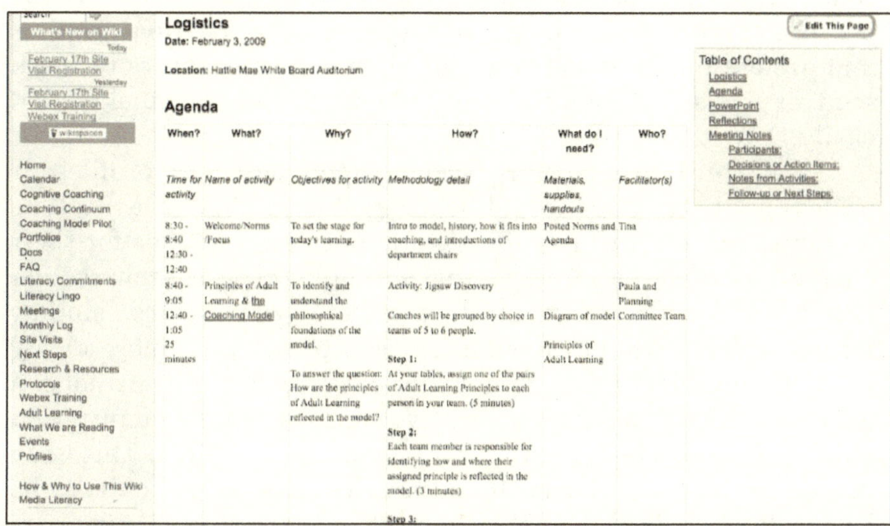

Personal Portfolios

Some businesses have found it useful to allow employees to create "personal profiles" as separate wiki pages. When employees edit articles, their edits are tracked and linked back to the employees' personal profiles. This could be very useful in education organizations for several purposes. First, from a supervisory perspective, employee contributions to organizational knowledge can be easily tracked by viewing an employee's editing history on the wiki. This would be helpful for annual professional evaluations and when administrators are making decisions about assignments to leadership positions.

A second use of these "personal profiles" would be related to a decision-making process around the development of specific teams. For example, if an administrator wanted to create an ad hoc committee to research and make recommendations about a proposed initiative, the administrator could perform a search on the wiki for key terms related to the initiative. Employee "personal profiles" which are set up to also serve as Professional Portfolios for each employee, contain those key terms that will show up in the search results. From these search results, the administrator can generate a list of employees who have worked on similar committees or projects and who may have an interest in the proposed initiative. In other words, employee personal profiles and professional portfolios would allow administrators to track staff expertise, skills, and professional interests quickly and easily.

A third use is more social. Open personal profiles or professional portfolios would be accessible to all staff as well as administration. Staff members could perform searches for their particular areas of interest and through these search results they can locate other staff members who share similar interests. This would allow employees to network more easily with like-minded peers which increases collegiality, and can lead to a much more collaborative culture where faculty and staff feel more connected to their colleagues. While this may not seem like a priority to administrators and faculty who belong to the "Baby Boom" cohort, it is a priority for members of the Generation Y cohort and for many members of the Generation X cohort who are accustomed to social networking through online tools such as Facebook.com, MySpace.com, and LinkedIn.com. Members of Generation Y and many members of Generation X are inherently collaborative and networked due to their experiences with interactive online social tools. Veteran educators and educational leaders should not dismiss these social uses of technology as unimportant to employee motivation and job satisfaction — they will become increasingly more important as more members of Generation Y enter the profession (see SIDEBAR – Generational Dynamics).

Creation of a personal profile or professional portfolio would be an excellent activity during an introductory professional development session on the use of an organization-wide enterprise wiki. You may find it helpful to provide faculty and staff with some minimal guidelines on what to include on their personal profile or professional portfolio page.

Profiles may include:

- Name and contact information
- Current position, campus/department, and professional interests
- Brief resume/CV
- Current projects or teaching assignments
- Links to personal websites (online professional portfolios, LinkedIn.com profiles, professional blog, etc.)

SIDEBAR - Generational Dynamics

Incentives and motivators for Generation X and Generation Y are different from those for the Boomers. According to authors William Strauss and Neil Howe, members of Generation X seek to build strong families and are reluctant to sacrifice that goal for the sake of their career. Generation Xers differ from their parents (the Boomers) in their unwillingness to accept a corporate culture that demands excessive hours and energy from its employees, and they prefer work environments that are generally more flexible, more "networked," and less bureaucratic (Strauss & Howe, 1997). Not much has been written in the media about this issue and its impact on our educational systems, but the media has published extensive coverage of the "Generation Gap" in the corporate workplace. Educational leaders need to be aware of the shift that is occurring in order to develop, nurture, and retain potential future leaders from both the Generation X and Generation Y cohorts.

Thanks to their early life experiences as latchkey children, children of divorce, and blended families, Generation X has a "reactive mindset" that values independence and eschews institutionalism. They are suspicious of traditional forms of authority and want no part of this system (Strauss & Howe, 1997). Generation X leaders are more likely to adopt "servant leadership" traits and to work closely with members of Generation Y to integrate appropriate technologies that transform their work, their workplace, and their organizations in ways that are more conducive to flatter, more democratic and collaborative environments. Yes, Generation X as a whole is more interested in their families than money, and they will collaborate with Generation Y to achieve a work environment that allows for the balance that both generations seek in their lives.

Some readers may be thinking that this is just simple generational stereotyping. While it is true that some Generation Xers think and act more like Boomers and some

Boomers behave and act more like Generation Xers or Yers, these personal and professional characteristics are generally true for the vast majority of each of these generational cohorts, and these characteristics do impact the modern workplace. We can look around us and see this in action without ever knowing the generational dynamics theory proposed by Strauss, Howe, and other researchers.

School districts are concerned about the number of Boomer leaders who will be retiring within the next several years. Unless current systems and structures change dramatically, the potential up-and-coming leaders will "opt out" of the leadership roles as they are currently structured. Perhaps this will be good for education. Perhaps tomorrow's leaders will "drop out" only to go out and, in the Generation X entrepreneurial way, finally engage in that education "reinvention" that Tony Wagner proposes (Wagner, Kegan, et al, 2006). Many educators already believe that Generation Y (and the Homeland Generation) students will eventually reinvent education to suit their own needs (through the use of emerging technologies), and perhaps those students will find willing leaders in Generation X who will enthusiastically help them with that reinvention.

Current educational leaders can harness the enthusiasm and energy of the Generation X and Generation Y cohorts by encouraging and facilitating the use of social networking and web-based tools such as wikis throughout the organization. A "new teacher wiki" might be a great supplement to more traditional induction methods, and school or districtwide policies can be placed on the wiki in draft form to encourage and invite input from all staff members before finalization of the plans or policies. Rather than fear the changes and the technology, all educational leaders — regardless of their generational cohort — must embrace and own the use of these new tools in all aspects of professional work.

Wikis for Professional Learning and Faculty Collaboration

Professional Learning Communities

In *Professional Learning Communities at Work,* Rick Dufour and Robert Eaker state that "educators seeking to create more effective schools must transform them into professional learning communities." Dufour and Eaker define Professional Learning Communities (PLCs) as teams that are focused on three priorities: Learning, Collaborative Culture, and Results. While PLCs do allow for a collaborative focus on learning and results, Dufour and Eaker warn that "the devil is in the details" in that educators are often given ambiguous, often conflicting advice on how to go about implementing PLCs on their campuses (DuFour and Eaker, 1998). Not only is the concept often ambiguous to many educators — especially when the logistics of implementation are equally ambiguous to administrators — but the daily practice of operating in PLCs is fraught with issues around effective meeting facilitation and the ever-increasing paper load that comes with developing "collaborative plans" and "collaborative common assessments." Too often, the knowledge and work of the PLCs remains isolated within the team "silos," never seeing the light of day. From an administrative perspective, monitoring the work of the PLCs can be demanding and frustrating due to accessibility of the PLC documentation. If ever there was a need for more effective "knowledge management" on our school campuses, it is now with the growing trend of PLC implementation across the country.

Wikis allow for a more productive collaborative culture focused on learning and results as PLCs can use wiki pages to create and monitor S.M.A.R.T. goals and action plans, develop common lessons, cross-reference lessons with collaboratively developed curriculum documents, and develop and record meeting agendas, notes, and action items. The use of a wiki will not replace the valuable face-to-face interactions of regular PLC meetings but it can help make those face-to-face meetings more productive and meaningful by allowing team members to immediately record decisions, plans, and meeting notes in addition to providing a perpetually accessible record of PLC work. Additionally, administrators will appreciate the ease of accessibility that they will have to the work of each PLC through the wiki. While specific student information should not be included on any wiki pages, a significant portion of the work generated by the team can be shared and archived through the wiki.

Another one of the challenges with trying to implement PLCs on a campus is that some schools have some teachers who have no content area colleagues with whom to collaborate. While this is rare, it is a situation that does occur and the professional learning needs of these teachers must also be addressed. In these instances, a wiki would provide a medium for "virtual PLCs" to exist across a district or region for teachers of specialized subjects.

Critical Friends Groups

According to the National School Reform Faculty (NSRF), a Critical Friends Group (CFG) is defined as "a professional learning community consisting of approximately 8-12 educators who come together voluntarily at least once a month for about 2 hours. Group members are committed to improving their practice through collaborative learning." Conceived of and developed originally by the Annenberg Institute for School Reform, CFGs emerged in the early 1990s and have since spread across the country and around the world as an effective professional learning experience for reflective education professionals. At the NSRF Annual Winter Meeting in January of 2009, the first ever *Moving CFGs Online* pre-conference session was convened. As a result of the discussions and work conducted during this pre-conference session, a group of experienced CFG Coaches are embarking on a year-long exploration of conducting CFG meetings online using a variety of Web 2.0 and electronic communication tools. A wiki will be one of the many ways that this group will collaborate on shared learning, and wikis in general are being explored for their use not only for virtual teams but also for supplementing more traditional face-to-face CFG experiences.

The Houston Independent School District Literacy Support Network wiki is being used for everything from collecting resources, keeping meeting agendas and notes to embedding training modules and reflection forms. This network has also experimented successfully with the use of wikis during regular weekly meetings as a way to capture meeting notes and as a replacement for the traditional Post-It chart paper. Small groups of network members are able to "scribe" their collective work on separate wiki pages — using the wiki pages in place of post-it chart paper (saving money and time), which makes the collective work immediately accessible to the entire network.

Other team collaboration ideas

The University of Southern California's Center for Scholarly Technology wrestled with implementation of blogs and wikis in the classroom across USC, and over the past few years they have examined their implementation practices to refine how and why wikis are being used across their campus. In the Fall semester of 2005, the CST identified six general approaches for how wikis could be implemented around campus, and in addition to the classroom/student uses of wikis for student journaling, personal portfolios, and collaborative project knowledge bases, the CST also found the wikis useful for faculty practices such as research coordination and collaboration, curricular and cross-disciplinary coordination, and conference and colloquia website/coordination (Higdon, 2005). While these faculty uses are somewhat different from faculty practice at K-12 campuses, they do resemble other practices such as the PLC collaborative work described earlier in this chapter as well as district level curriculum development practices and school or district activities and events.

A wiki can also be an effective place for a team to collaboratively share resources that they might otherwise not know that they have access to through each other. A specific example of this would be a situation where various members of the team are members of certain professional organizations and their membership provides them with access to online archives of the professional organizations' publications. If a member of the department team needs to get a copy of an article for research purposes from an organization of which he or she is not a member, he or she could access a wiki page that would list team members who do have access to this material.

Lesson Plans

Wikis can be used as a method for storing and sharing lesson plans. In many schools, teachers are required to develop lesson plans and submit them to their supervising administrator. In a school that uses a wiki for communication and knowledge management, teachers can post lesson plans to a wiki space designated specifically for them. Administrators can easily pull up the wiki each week to see updated lesson plans. This would result in either a reduction of emails or a reduction in printed copies depending on how a school currently handles this requirement. This also meets the PLC principle of transparent professional practice while serving as an excellent way to capture the tacit knowledge of veteran teachers.

The structure of a wiki used for lesson plans can vary according to the needs of the specific campus. Pages can be structured by date, by teacher, or by subject area, with teachers posting as needed in the appropriate page. Administrators or other teachers can easily locate weekly lessons by using the search function of the wiki to find lessons posted by specific teachers or from specific subject areas. Administrators who use RSS aggregators can easily subscribe to the RSS feed for that particular wiki in order to get weekly updates sent directly to their RSS aggregator.

Curriculum Mapping

As the wiki begins to "house" lesson plans, the school or district can implement the use of wiki for the purpose of Curriculum Mapping. Curriculum Maps allow faculty and administration to see how the entire scope and sequence of all curriculum areas relate to one another. Curriculum Maps are helpful to interdisciplinary teams who are interested in aligning all curricula horizontally and vertically across multiple disciplines. Each content area can create separate wiki pages for each major unit or in smaller units if the team chooses, and these units can be indexed on a central wiki page that contains a matrix that shows the order and content focus of all units. Each content focus title links back to the original page, but the matrix allows users to view all the curricula at a glance.

This structure enables the curriculum team to identify gaps in sequencing order across the curriculum while also strengthening the development of professional learning communities that learn together through their collaborative work. For example, through the mapping process a team might notice that an eighth grade science unit relies on students knowing certain math content before the math content is taught in the 8th grade math area. The awareness of this misalignment provides an excellent opportunity for interdisciplinary collaboration, and hopefully provides an outcome that results in a more coherent and better-aligned curriculum across the board.

Grading Periods (right) Subject Areas (below)	1	2	3	4	5	6
Algebra I	Patterns & Multiple Representations Proportional Reasoning	Algebraic Properties & Solving Linear Equations Proportional Reasoning & Algebraic Properties & Solving Linear Equations	Rate of Change & Intercepts Writing & Graphing Linear Equations Line of Best Fit Systems of Linear Equations	Systems of Equations & Inequalities Polynomials & Exponents Quadratic Functions pt. 1	Quadratic Functions pt. 2 Probability & Statistics	Exponential Functions & Inverse Variations Bridge to Geometry
English I		Fiction Reading - Tragedy	The Media Coming of Age	Assessment Practice	Marxism, Totalitarianism, Communism Historical Fiction - Animal Farm	
IPC	Scientific Method, Measurement, and Safety Force & Motion	Machines & Efficiency Heat Electricity	Sound and Waves Light Energy Resources	Properties & Classifications of Matter Physical & Chemical Changes Atomic Structure	Bonding & Periodic Table Chemical Reactions	Solutions Acids & Bases Nuclear Energy
World Geography	Patterns in Our Physical World Patterns in Our Human world	US and Canada Mexico, Central America, and the Carribean	South America Europe	Russia and the CIS Africa	Southwest Asia South Asia	East & Southeast Asia The Land Down Under - Australia, New Zealand, Antarctica

This example shows how a matrix may be created on a wiki to help educators with curriculum mapping. Each of the unit topics are linked to pages that provide more in-depth information while the matrix allows for a “big picture” view of the entire curriculum.

Professional Development

One challenge that schools and districts face is a shortage of time and money to send everyone to conferences and workshops. A second related challenge is how to facilitate the sharing of knowledge gained at conferences and workshops when faculty and staff members are able to attend. Wikis can be very useful in the collection and dissemination of conference materials and knowledge.

A wiki can be set up so that each conference or workshop attendee can add articles as they attend sessions, or to highlight new ideas gathered in informal discussions and scouting the vendor floor. The wiki may also be a place to collect ideas for a "mini-conference" that the team will organize when they return to campus, and the team can draft the mini-conference agenda directly onto a page in the wiki. One page of the wiki might also be a place for the team to collect a "wish list" of stuff that they see on the vendor floor that they are interested in learning more about for use on campus. A conference or workshop wiki provides solutions for attendees who need to take notes and collect new knowledge and ideas, and provides solutions for leaders who want to ensure that funds expended are beneficial to the whole organization when the information is shared through the wiki. See the SIDEBAR – Tag-Teaming Conferences for an example.

Site-based professional development can also benefit from the use of a wiki. Faculty and staff members who facilitate on-site professional development can use a wiki to plan the sessions and agendas, and can either use sections of the wiki as the informational handouts or upload .PDF copies of handouts directly into the wiki for attendees to download to their own computers. To extend this idea even further, facilitators might allow attendees to create their own pages within the wiki for the purpose of taking notes during the sessions. By adding their pages to a page designated as a "directory," all notes are shared by all attendees, which allows for increased sharing of knowledge and insights. The notes along with the session agendas and handouts are all contained within one wiki and become part of the organizational knowledge "archive."

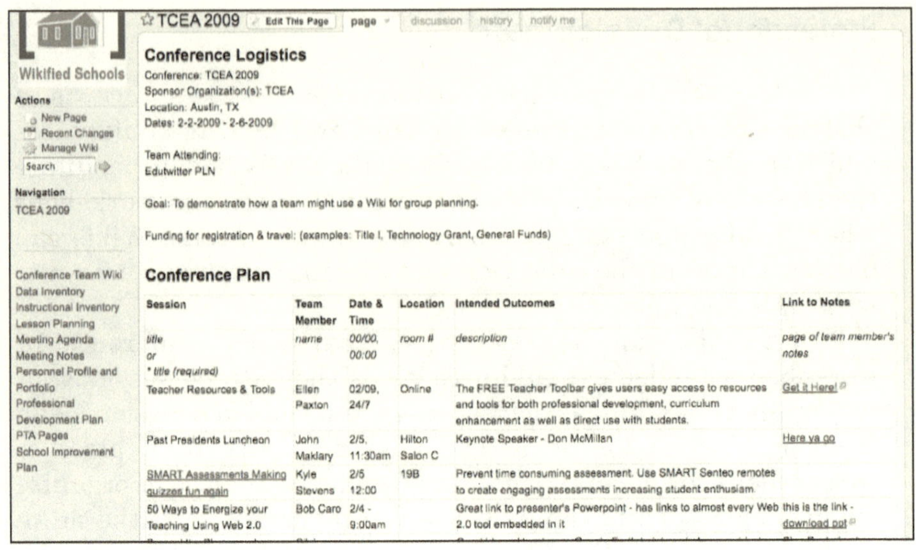

A school team can use a wiki to organize their notes and resources gathered from attending a conference making it easy for faculty to access the information for professional development.

For leaders who want better ways to document site-based professional development — especially for grant or funding purposes — what better way to do it than through a wiki? The wiki also becomes a professional development session “sign-in sheet” as the list of “recent changes” automatically provides an accurate accounting of all participants as they create and edit their own note pages.

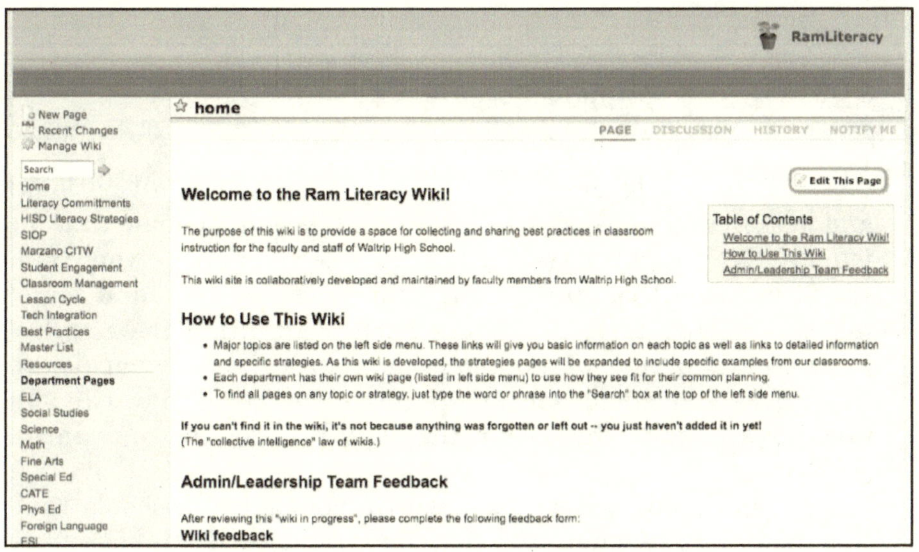

A wiki can be used in place of a 3-ring binder for faculty resources. This wiki was developed on one campus to replace the more traditional "Teacher Instructional Resources" manual that faculty usually received at the beginning of the year. All faculty members can edit the content to add specific examples of each instructional strategy from their classroom which makes the entire resource much more dynamic than the more traditional binder which could only be changed once per year.

SIDEBAR - Tag-Teaming Conferences

It is nearly impossible to send everyone to all national and regional conferences — there just is not enough time or money. Even if you have the money, there's no way you could get everyone off campus in the middle of the year and many teachers choose to teach summer school (limiting their ability to take advantage of summer conferences). So what is an innovative and caring school administrator to do? How can you take advantage of these learning opportunities for your entire staff?

Time and money. The two things that all schools wish they had more of when it comes to planning and implementing effective professional development. As a campus administrator I received those colorful and intriguing flyers in my mailbox almost weekly and I always wished I could send my entire staff to several conferences and institutes each year. Unfortunately, I needed my teachers to be in the classroom with our students, and there was never enough money to send everyone anyway. So why even dream?

Dreaming provides an opportunity find creative solutions to our problems. In this case, our campus was able to develop a solution that allowed us to take advantage of some of the conference offerings while also sharing new learning with the entire campus. Using a variety of funds (general funds, Title I, some grants, etc.) we made the decision to send a team to about three conferences per year — one in the summer, one in the fall, and one in the spring. The strategy includes three very important components:

1. Send a different team to each conference or institute (use a full faculty roster to keep track of this) and be sure to include a representative from each department as well as an administrator.
2. Team members must make a commitment to giving a presentation or setting up some kind of professional development for the whole staff within four months after

returning from the conference.

3. Provide time or a schedule to support the on-campus training provided by the conference attendees.

The most effective strategy that we have found for #3 (providing time) has been to create a mini-conference with a variety of "concurrent sessions" that the staff can choose to attend on a full professional development day. This takes some pre-planning, which can easily be accomplished with the use of wiki, and the results are well worth the efforts.

Large conferences usually provide a tentative conference planner online or in print before the opening day of the conference. By carefully using the conference planner to select strands or specific sessions the team can plan their session before leaving campus. The team can complete the planning by using a table on a wiki page. If six people attend the conference, and those six people are able to sit through three to four sessions per day for three days, the total sessions attended equals fifty-four to seventy-two different sessions... that is a lot of learning! If all the session notes are captured on a wiki, your team returns to the campus with a tremendous amount of new knowledge to share with the staff. All of that new knowledge is instantly available through the wiki. In fact, during the conference, non-attendees can access the wiki daily to see what new knowledge the team is gathering each day.

The emergence of blogging and other Web 2.0 tools increases the opportunities to share new learning with other faculty who are not able to attend the conferences. Perhaps you could have a "home team" of faculty members who attend the conference virtually. This "home team" could aggregate RSS feeds from conference bloggers to do any or all the following:

- collect information on a variety of sessions or specific strands
- collect information from presenter websites and wikis
- communicate information back to conference attendees (from their own campus)
- conduct additional research on specific topics of interest to the whole team and begin compiling resources for use when

everyone is back on campus

This "home team" may consist of faculty who are interested but are not able to attend for a variety of reasons — young children at home during the summer, teaching summer school, or vital core staff who cannot be out of the classroom during the school year. Two key components of this strategy include the Team Blog and the Team Wiki.

The Team Blog

Each team member can be an author and he or she can use the blog to do live-blogging sessions, post photos, or just publish daily summaries of their learning at the conference. "Home Team" members can subscribe to the blog and get daily updates from their colleagues who are at the conference.

The Team Wiki

Similar to the blog idea above, a team wiki could be set up so that each team member could add articles as he or she attends sessions or to highlight new ideas gathered in informal discussions and scouting the vendor floor. The wiki could also be a place to collect ideas for a "mini-conference" that the team will organize when they return to campus, and the team could draft the mini-conference agenda directly onto a page in the wiki. One page of the wiki could also be a place for the team to collect a "wish list" of stuff that they see on the vendor floor that they are interested in learning more about for use on campus.

You can combine both ideas above and link both through linked RSS feeds (blog includes RSS feed from wiki and wiki includes RSS feed from blog). As team members attend sessions, all their notes are collected in one (or two) places and the entire team has instant access to everyone else's notes. This saves time and increases the shared learning that can occur during attendance at such a large conference.

Other tools to consider include Google Docs (and Spreadsheets and Presentations), Del.icio.us and Diigo (for Social Bookmarking), and Twitter.

Wikis for Home-to-School Communications and Collaboration

The National PTA recommends that schools and parents be "on the same page," share information, and form a communication team that consists of parents, teachers, students, and school administrators in order to improve home-school communication (National PTA, 2000). A wiki can facilitate this process by allowing the communication team to collaborate on the development of home-school communication policies and practices.

A PTA/PTO wiki can incorporate a variety of components that include anything from pages used to collaboratively plan meeting agendas and school events to providing a space for the PTA/PTO and school to share current announcements and upcoming events. Calendars can be built into the wiki space to improve communication of upcoming events to the broader community.

The school can use the wiki space to publish information to parents including tips and advice on how they can support student learning at home and outside of the school day. Pages on the wiki space can also be dedicated to planning volunteer activities on the campus, soliciting input from parents on school decision-making, and providing contact information on faculty and staff to parents and the community.

If the school is in the process of improving or increasing its community business partnerships, the wiki would also be an excellent medium for providing information to prospective business partners on how they can support the school and the benefits that the school can provide to the partner.

School administrators can increase the use of the wiki by providing parents with access to computers during the school day. Some schools have created "Parent Centers" on their campus that are open during school hours to any parents who do not have internet access at home. The Parent Center, which is usually located in a small room or office space, has internet-connected computers (anywhere from five to fifteen) that parents can use for research, job searching, resume writing, and other personal business activities. The Parent Center can also be used to host events such as "Coffee with the

Principal" and technology training sessions for parents and community members.

The Westlake High School PTO in Austin, Texas has a PTO wiki (hosted on PBwiki) for communicating with the school community. The information contained within the Westlake PTO wiki includes recent news, contact information for PTO officers, volunteer opportunities, fund raising activities, information on special PTO sponsored projects, and meeting minutes. On the home page of their wiki, the PTO states that one of its reasons for using electronic media is to communicate "greener":

> "We have historically made copies of PTO minutes and meetings agendas available at our meetings, but these sets of paper copies waste resources and consume PTO funds to produce. Let's do better! Beginning this year, we will make minutes and agendas available via professional development, so you can read them, save them, review them online, and come to meetings just a little better prepared!"

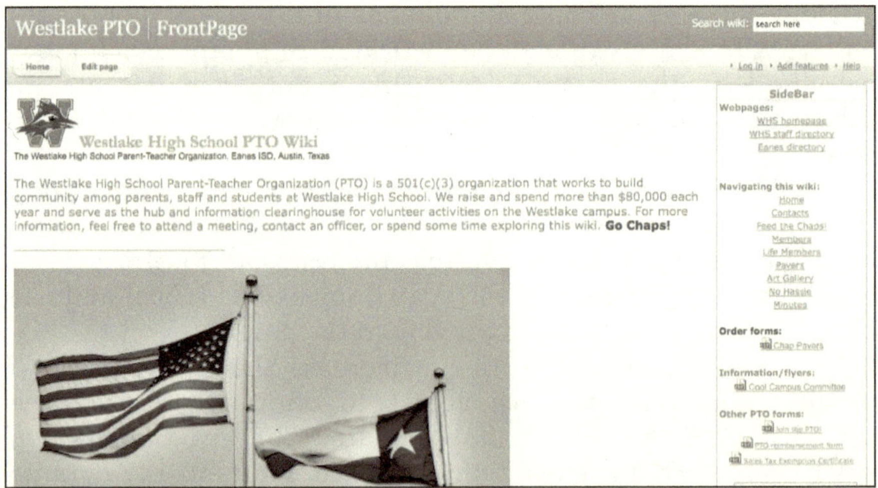

The Westlake PTO wiki includes basic membership information, details on fundraisers, and documents used throughout the year.

In summary, uses for PTA/PTO wikis may include:

- Sharing mission statements, officer profiles, and contact info
- Keeping members up to date on what is happening with the organization.
- Creating calendar pages to track all PTO events during the school year.
- Compiling and sharing fundraising plans, ideas, and event feedback.
- Posting meeting agendas, notes, and tracking follow-up action items.
- Creating volunteer sign-up pages for events, errands, etc.
- Posting picture galleries, slideshows, and clips of PTO events.
- Sending messages via the wiki to share news, solicit information, or collect feedback.
- Easily attaching copies of all standard forms (membership, volunteer forms, etc.)

  Source: WetPaint

Wikis in the Classroom

The concept of using wikis in classroom instruction has been covered extensively in a number of other books, blogs, and websites. Educators around the world are already using wikis and discovering their value for engaging students in real-world collaborative learning with 21st-Century tools. A simple Google search for "wikis in education" brings up more than 19,000,000 results! Most arguments for the use of wikis in the classroom revolve around the issue of preparing students for global communication and collaboration, which will surely be a component of the 21st-Century workplace that they will enter upon leaving school. In this section we want to focus instead on the basic literacy skills that can be developed through appropriate use of wikis in the classroom as well as the advanced 21st-Century Literacy skills that wikis require of users — skills that students will develop through the use of wikis in their learning experiences.

The United States National Institute for Literacy provides the following definition for literacy:

> "The Workforce Investment Act of 1998 defines literacy as "an individual's ability to read, write, speak in English, compute and solve problems at levels of proficiency necessary to function on the job, in the family of the individual and in society." This is a broader view of literacy than just an individual's ability to read, the more traditional concept of literacy. As information and technology have increasingly shaped our society, the skills we need to function successfully have gone beyond reading, and literacy has come to include the skills listed in the current definition."

By the definition provided by the United States government, literacy is defined much more broadly than just reading and writing. The Houston Independent School District adopted a definition of literacy that included "reading, writing, listening, speaking, and thinking" (Houston Independent School District, 2005). Those terms encompass nearly anything we do when we interact with other people or with information whether it is in print, on the web, or incorporated in static visuals, video, or audio. In the past few years we have begun to hear terms such as 21st-Century Literacy Skills, and the implications in the use of this term is that the skills that students need today are different from what they needed yesterday. Students today operate in a world very different from the one in which we grew up, but while the media that students engage with may be different, the media still require students to use skills that apply to all old and new media — the ability to read, decode, comprehend, write fluently and clearly, to articulate their thoughts orally as well as in writing, and to listen for understanding. These essential basic literacy skills have not changed. One can argue that hyper-text transforms reading from a linear activity into a nonlinear activity, but in some ways reading nonlinear hyper-text on the internet is not so different from the "choose your path" fiction that we read as adolescents.

What is not debatable is the sad fact that adult literacy remains a serious problem in our society with recent studies indicating that 1 in 7 adults are functionally illiterate (Toppo, 2009). Without drastic changes in the way we facilitate student learning, this statistic will not change. The fact is that in too many schools we are still using teaching methods that resulted in this high rate of illiteracy, and unfortunately we are using these methods with students who are even less engaged with the curriculum than previous generations. Even more daunting is the fact that literacy needs have increased and the skills considered basic for employment, college, careers, and even the military have increased beyond what was considered basic for older generations. Technology has changed the way we work as well as the way we learn regardless of the debate around the concept of "21st-Century Literacy & Skills." As Judith Irwin (2007) explains in *Taking Action on Adolescent Literacy*:

> Understanding the relationship between literacy and technology means that schools should examine:
>
> - what types of academic literacy habits and skills are needed to prepare students for the future they face;
> - how contexts for conducting research, learning, reading, and writing have changed because of the available technologies; and
> - how assignments, teaching goals, and understandings about literacy have shifted.

As I was describing how a wiki works to one of my colleagues who specializes in adolescent literacy, she looked at me with astonishment as I explained the process of editing and revising and said "That in itself is an entirely new literacy!" She was referring to the aspect of wiki editing that allows users to review all edits made on the wiki and to be able to track participation as well as to revert to previous edits if needed. She realized that the ability to understand the structure and function of a wiki was something that would have to be explicitly taught to users before they could effectively use the wiki in a fluent manner.

If we consider the fact that wiki use in corporate America is becoming more widespread, then there are arguments for using wikis in the classroom in order to explicitly teach students "wiki literacy" in preparation for their future careers that will surely demand online collaboration. Additionally, if designed properly, projects that require the use of a wiki (by the students) will also help to build critical-thinking skills as well as editing and revising skills. A wiki can be a powerful tool for helping students develop skills in critical analysis and review of information. They can "fact-check" the contributions of others and make immediate changes if necessary. For the teacher — as well as the students — the structure of the wiki allows for facilitator-monitored or self-monitored participation. As all changes are tracked by user, any user can easily see if all members of a group are participating equally in the creation of the knowledge.

In addition to the benefits for building adolescent literacy skills described above, teachers can also use wikis for more administrative tasks in and outside of the classroom. This accomplishes two goals: building teacher capacity in the use of new technologies and providing professional models of technology use for students. Teachers can use wikis for:

- Class notes and lesson summaries
- Parental and student communication
- Handouts
- Course syllabus
- Course links and resource notes
- School or class calendar
- Collaborative note-taking
- Concept introduction and exploratory projects
- Dissemination of important classroom learning beyond the classroom
- Teacher information page
- Student-authored books
- School newspaper

Security issues

Despite the common perception that wikis are open to the world for viewing and editing, all wikis allow information to be secured at the page or article level. This means that certain sections of the wiki can be open to the public — parents and students — for the purpose of sharing curriculum and lesson plans, while more sensitive information such as common assessment drafts can be secured and accessible only to relevant staff members. The public space of the wiki, especially that containing information such as curriculum and lesson plans, can be "read only" to parents and students in order to prevent pranks and vandalism by students.

Reflection Questions

In what areas could you use a wiki in your school or district?
What are the challenges you face for each of those purposes?
What supports are currently in place that would make wiki adoption easier?

Chapter 5: How – Making it Work in Your Organization

"The adoption and diffusion of an innovation within an institution does not guarantee its successful integration into the curriculum or its continued use."
- V.H. Carr Jr.

If you build it, they will collaborate, right? Not so fast. As with any new initiative, adoption and implementation will fail without an effective approach. A top-down mandate in and of itself will not be sufficient, especially considering the wide range of technology skill and comfort-levels of the entire staff. A bottom-up "grassroots" effort will also fail without proper and appropriate administrative support. A balance between the two is needed for organization-wide adoption of wiki use.

A careful analysis of how wikis have been successfully implemented on a variety of K-12 and college campuses reveals that the most successful implementations were those where the users were allowed to shape the structure of the wikis and make decisions on how to use the wikis to fulfill their own individual or team objectives. These successful implementations, while supported by administration, were not mandated in a top-down manner (Lamb, 2004). This is an important recommendation that bears repeating: Administrators and organization leaders must resist the urge to dictate or impose too much structure on the wiki as this can inhibit or stall adoption of the wiki by faculty and staff.

Figure 5.1: Technology Adoption Model

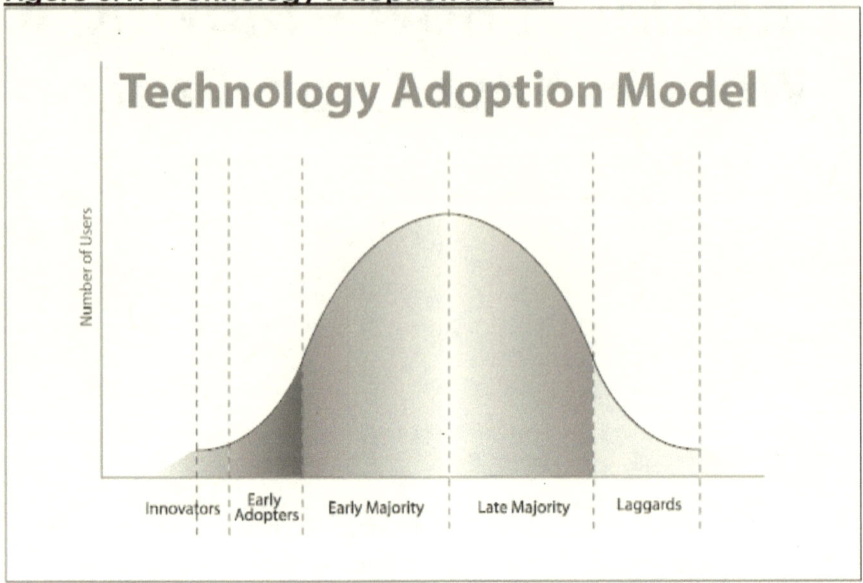

We can reflect on efforts to implement email use within education organizations over the past 10 to 15 years. In some cases, there are still pockets of practice today where information or items that could easily be emailed to colleagues are instead shared in print form, or worse, in lengthy "pointless" meetings. Email has still not successfully infiltrated all possible communication areas within our schools and districts, and researchers have found that some educators are slow to adopt email and other technologies due to ineffective or nonexistent training, the acceleration of emergence of new technology trends, the availability of easy-to-use applications or systems, hands-on experience, administrative support, and individual technology anxiety level (Shelley, 1998). Reflecting on this, no one should expect wiki adoption and implementation to happen overnight. Keep in mind the Technology Adoption Model (Figure 5.1) and remember that some staff may never use the wiki. However, there are steps that schools and organizations can take to foster a climate more conducive to wiki adoption. In order to successfully implement wiki use, we must first understand "lessons learned" by other schools that have taken on the process of implementation and adoption of wikis.

Dos & Don'ts

Do provide access to the wiki outside of district or school intranets.

Adoption will happen more quickly if staff can access the wiki from any location and not just from the office or campus. Password protection can be used for sensitive information. The ultimate goal of using a wiki is to improve communication and collaboration in such a way that there is also an improvement in productivity. Limiting users to access only in the office defeats that purpose, and will ultimately result in a failed attempt at wiki adoption. In order to promote adoption, it should be easily accessible and easy to use. Keep it simple.

Do encourage "grass-roots" adoption.

If your entire organization or school is not yet ready to plunge into system-wide wiki use, allow smaller groups or teams to create their own wikis. These wikis can serve as models for future wikis and all the content can be easily transferred to a system-wide enterprise wiki when or if one is implemented.

Don't impose an overly strict structure to the wiki.

Do allow employees to define a structure that meets their needs as often as possible. Start with a skeletal structure and allow employees the flexibility to change that structure as needed. The content that develops will ultimately dictate a certain structure but it is almost always nearly impossible to know exactly what that content will consist of and how it will need to be structured. Allow for an organic, flexible, and evolving structure from the beginning of wiki implementation.

Don't block access to free wiki sites such as Wikipedia, PBWiki, or WetPaint.

These free sites offer all staff members an easily accessible and easy-to-use space where they can explore how to use wikis by creating their own for personal use. A staff member may want to create their own personal wiki to use for their own organization, project management, or lesson planning outside of the district or school provided wiki. Resist the urge to control wiki use. These personal explorations allow users to learn more and understand the wiki much more deeply.

Do get permission to publish images of students and colleagues.

This is a no-brainer for legal reasons — especially when students are involved. While it normally is not necessary to request permission of colleagues, it is always courteous to do so.

Do provide praise and encouragement for ANY participation, then, praise and encouragement for meaningful participation.

We are human. We like to receive a "pat on the back" when we participate in ways that add value to the whole. When we receive this kind of acknowledgment we are encouraged to continue participating because we feel supported, and we feel as if our voice and our effort is valued.

Do insist on real names for username. Don't allow for anonymous edits or comments. Do set a positive, constructive tone early.

Online etiquette is very important because we lose the visual and verbal cues that are present in face-to-face settings. If everyone has not already learned how to communicate effectively in online text environments (for example, through email use) then they will need coaching in order to participate and collaborate in a positive and effective way with others on the team. Experienced users and leaders can model this communication behavior through their own participation. The use of real names helps provide the transparency necessary for safe, positive, and effective online collaboration and it holds people accountable for the content that they create.

Do start small, make edits together as a group the first time.

Group mentoring of new technologies can be as effective as one-on-one mentoring, but, of course, this is even more effective if paired with follow-up mentoring for employees who find the wiki challenging. Create a structured activity where everyone will be allowed the opportunity to create his or her personal profile page together in a meeting. This allows for a non-threatening introduction to basic wiki use and page editing.

Do promote the use of wiki over email and avoid the temptation to provide information in media other than the wiki.

Gently remind users to share information through the wiki rather than through email. Model the use of wiki for collaboration and the use of email for short, immediate messages that do not require intensive collaborative efforts. Do not provide alternative media or locations for information and content that is available on the wiki. When employees ask where they can find that information, remind them that it is on the wiki. The wiki should become the one-stop shop for all your documentation and information.

Don't take user experience for granted. Many of your users will not be web 2.0 savvy.

Be willing to accept that some of your employees have yet to accept email as the standard form of written communication across your organization. You cannot expect these employees to welcome another innovation that requires them to learn a new technology.

Do let go of the notion that physical presence is the only prerequisite for collaboration and productivity.

These new tools allow for asynchronous collaboration from any place, any time. In the 20th-Century workplace, employee productivity was measured in seat time much like learning in school. We must accept the fact that we are now able to work from anywhere at any time. This has been mentioned before but it bears repeating: Time is a scarce resource in our business, and it is frequently very difficult to coordinate face-to-face meeting times and locations with busy leadership teams who are taking care of the important school and/or district business. Much of our typical brainstorming and collaboration can take place asynchronously through wikis and other web-based tools. This is an uncomfortable shift for veteran educators who are accustomed to "face time," but it is a not-so-alien concept for younger, more "wired" workers.

SIDEBAR - Shift Happens - Now What?!

You've just watched "Did You Know" or a keynote by David Warlick — or you have just read this book — for the very first time. You feel your heart begin to race as panic sets in as you think: "My school is in no way prepared to help our students learn what they need for work and life in the this very different and constantly changing world... What should I do?!"

Too often, the initial response is to look for money to buy more computers. Some educational leaders may say "Let's make sure we have laptops in the hands of EVERY student!... SmartBoards in EVERY classroom!" While it is nice to have administrative support for new technology purchases, a "technology purchasing frenzy" is simply not the correct response to the realization that our schools are not doing enough to prepare students for their futures. This is about changing adult perspectives and adult behaviors to create student-centered classrooms that exemplify research-based best practices around learning. It is not about buying the latest, greatest, and most expensive tech toys on the market. Expensive technology in the hands of educators who have not made changes to their behaviors and instructional practice are no better than the traditional chalkboard, pencil, and paper. Even worse, expensive technology that the teachers see no use for will end up just collecting dust in a storage room.

The examples are endless: SmartBoards as expensive chalkboards, PowerPoint and media projectors as flashy and expensive overhead transparencies, computers as typewriters and calculators, Distance-learning labs that only get used for faculty or team meetings — or worse, as a nice empty room to use during testing week.

So what should we do when we realize that the world has changed for our students? Rather than immediately engage in a technology purchasing frenzy, take some time to begin discussions on your campus about how to transform your school into a place where teachers see themselves first as LEARNERS who are invested in improving their instructional practice through reflection and inquiry, and where students are more globally connected in a way that enhances and supports their individual learning. Collaborate with your faculty and staff — your learners — to learn more about how the world has changed, and what that means for our profession.

Locate the "early adopters" in your district/schools and bring them in to a conversation around change — recruit them to help spread change virally. Leaders may neglect to involve the early-adopters, and this is a mistake. The early adopters can help drive grass-roots efforts so that the change is not perceived as another top-down mandate or the next "new thing" that everyone can just ignore. However, "early adopters" are only part of the solution which should also include many conversations and professional learning around the implications of these changes and the use of these technologies in our work.

Change adult behaviors and practices first. Change the way you work together, the way you speak with each other. Change your vocabulary. Begin by redefining yourselves as learners rather than educators. Acknowledge that in order to prepare your students for their futures of the 21st-Century, all learners on your campus must be equally prepared for those futures, and commit to the belief that being "techno phobic" or "technology illiterate" is no longer an option for 21st-Century learners (and after you have redefined yourselves as learners, understand what that means for professional learning on your campus). Be firm about this — it should not be acceptable on your campus for anyone to say "I don't like technology" or "I'm just not very techie... can you do this for me?" Banish the phrase "Kids these days" from the vocabulary of everyone on your campus. While you are at it, you should also banish the phrase "My teaching methods have always worked and I'm not going to change just because these kids (fill in the blank)..."

Do not form a committee to "study this and bring back suggestions for change" — committees take too long and you just do not have time. Change needed to happen yesterday. Do not create a "pilot project" — same reasons for not forming a committee — it takes too long and change needed to happen yesterday. Pilot projects and committees can be useful if the results are used to move the organization forward. Too often pilot projects flounder and go nowhere while committees are formed and their suggestions ignored by the decision-makers. Too often the development of pilots and committees becomes a way for the administrators to say "see, we are taking action" without having to do the hard work of trying to implement deep, cultural change across the organization.

Do not purchase any new technology hardware until you have first ensured that your network is up-to-date and accessible. How many network drops are in each room? Do you have wireless access across your entire campus? Drops in every room and wireless access across the campus are "must-haves" before you start buying anything else!

Give your teachers time to "play" with Web 2.0 — to explore the use of Web 2.0 (blogs, wikis, Twitter, etc.) for their professional learning before they attempt to use the same tools in the classroom with students. In fact, put a moratorium on classroom use of blogs and wikis for at least four months until teachers have used them weekly for their own learning by reading and writing and connecting with other edublogging educators. Inform all new first-year learners (new teachers) on your campus that their "learning" is just beginning and will never end — and that it certainly did not end upon completion of all degree and certification requirements. Begin all interviews for new hires with "what is the most recent thing that you learned and how did you learn it?"

Understand that all this can and should happen in conjunction with other changes in professional practice such as Professional Learning Communities and Critical Friends Groups, and along with structural changes such as Smaller Learning Communities, varied student grouping strategies, and/or early college campuses. Transforming your school into a 21st-Century Learning Center does not mean that you throw out other initiatives and other research-based best practices.

Campus leaders should model the professional learning use of Web 2.0 tools through transparent blogging and wiki use with the faculty on a weekly basis. Begin putting all your professional "knowledge" on a wiki (accessible from anywhere — not on the campus intranet) and when your learners ask where they can find certain documents, policies, etc., smile and tell them "It's on the wiki!" Give your learners password-protected access to edit the wiki so that knowledge on your campus is collaboratively developed. This is as much about being transparent in your own learning and in your communication and collaborative decision-making with all your learners as it is about modeling the use of new tools.

Parents are also very important stakeholders who need to be a part of the conversations and the learning at all stages of the change process. Parents are also adult learners, and we can accomplish so much more in our schools when they are included.

If our students need to be educated for a globally connected workplace rather than educated for factory work (and yes, they do), collaborate with your learners to make system, process, and structural changes so that your school looks, feels, and functions less like a factory and more like a globally connected communications and learning center. Remember that the most important thing is a change in behaviors and practices — a change in pedagogy — not just buying new technology. Finally, when you do make technology purchases — provide support, provide support, provide support — and provide training. Provide training that is a model of effective instruction and learning practices. Create cheerleaders who will coach other professional learners and promote continual learning around changes in the world, economics, technology, and workforce trends that have an impact on our work as learning professionals.

This will require a complete rethinking of the way we structure our organizations. In a time of budget constraints it is difficult for district or school administrators to rethink staffing and time structures that allow for more professional learning time during the school day. But leaders must rethink both staffing and use of time if they hope to change this culture. Asking teachers to do this on their own time is only a "band-aid" at best. What is needed is leadership by people who understand the emotional and philosophical challenges of deep change and who are prepared to handle those challenges in a way that is respectful of everyone in the system.

Getting Started

Each school and district has its own particular culture and the characteristics of this culture will dictate the most successful process for implementing wiki use within the organization. The following step-by-step process is only provided as a general guide and is not intended to be a one-size-fits-all approach to implementation. You are encouraged to reflect on your own school, district, or department to determine the exact first steps for your team. Feel free to share your "recipe" on the book wiki (http://wikifiedschools.com) to provide other readers with additional examples.

Step 1: Decide on use of a wiki hosting service or a stand-alone wiki installed on your servers

There are so many options available and your first step is going to involve deciding which of those options is best for the needs of your organization. In some cases a mixture of free hosting on "wiki farms" and stand-alone software may be the preferred option. Free wiki hosting services, or wiki farms, include Wikispaces.com, PBWiki.com, and WetPaint.com. Stand-alone software can include purchased packages that come with support or free open-source software that will require on-site staff who are able to install, setup, and support the wiki. Free open-source packages include MediaWiki (used by Wikipedia and familiar to most people), TikiWiki (http://info.tikiwiki.org/tiki-index.php), and PhpWiki (http://phpwiki.sourceforge.net/) to name a few.

You should begin this decision process by deciding which features you need or want to have on your wiki then conduct research to identify the hosting service or software that meets those needs. A list of resources that will aid you in your research is located in the Recommended Reading and Resources section of this book, and on the book wiki: http://wikifiedschools.com. Your selection at this point will dictate your choice of hosting options:

1. Install the wiki software or "engine" of your choice on your server, which is either your own hardware, or a server that you rent from a web host. In this option you are responsible

for and in control of all aspects of installation, maintenance, upgrades, and support.

2. Create a wiki on any of the free hosting wiki farms. Someone else is generally in control of installation, maintenance, upgrades, and support. You are able to focus on content, organization, business process, and social functions of the wiki.

Step 2: Informal, grassroots implementation

Allow early-adopters to start using the wiki in their departments or teams. These users will be the most likely to invest the time and energy to contributing content, organizing the content, and determining the best ways to use the wiki in your school or district when you are ready to scale up.

Step 3: Action Research – document best practices specific to your organization, and determine what works and what doesn't work for your school or district

Document your processes as the wiki develops and allow your early-adopters group to develop user guides for your organization. Their experience will prove to be incredibly valuable as you begin to determine what will work best in your work environment. These best practices can even be documented right inside the wiki on a "best practices" page or space within the wiki.

Step 4: Focus, Structure, and Guidelines

Before rolling out to other users, determine a focus for your wiki, decide on any kind of basic structure for content (keeping in mind that this will change as the wiki grows), and develop some basic community guidelines for content creation, editing, and user interactions. Your grassroots group will be valuable in this stage of development and implementation.

Step 5: Roll out to other users with training, support, and mentoring

As with any technology integration, the implementation of a school or district wiki will require the investment of time for training, support, and mentoring. Your early-adopters can serve as informal mentors for new users, and this is an excellent way for follow-up support after initial training.

Step 6: Nurture, encourage, and celebrate successes and innovative use

The often overlooked step in any technology implementation project is the most important step for "growing" the technology use. Grow your wiki by nurturing and encouraging your users, then take time to recognize success and innovative uses of the wiki. Has someone learned a new way to embed other media or developed an effective way of using wiki pages with teacher teams? Highlight those accomplishments on a "recent news" section of the wiki, and encourage those users to share their accomplishments through a workshop that they can facilitate to teach others what they have learned or developed.

Logistics & Use

As stated in the previous section, school leaders interested in using wikis in their organizations have several options from which to choose including many free options that are useful for those who are just beginning to explore wiki use. The easiest way to get started is, of course, to create a free wiki on one of the popular wiki farms such as Wikispaces (http://wikispaces.com), PBWiki (http://pbwiki.com), and WetPaint (http://wetpaint.com). These three wiki-hosting farms are simple to use for beginners and provide adequate functionality for most knowledge management and planning uses on school campuses. A more technical solution is MediaWiki, a free open-source software package that can be installed on a web server. MediaWiki offers a great deal more functionality, but requires more technical expertise to install, maintain, and use. In this chapter we will look at these four options to explore their features. We will also discuss basics of using wikis along with syntax used to create wiki pages and "wiki etiquette."

Wikispaces (http://wikispaces.com), one of the most widely used wiki-hosts in education, provides several levels of subscriptions for users. The basic, free level includes Google Adsense ads, but Wikispaces has generously waived this for educational users. PBWiki (http://pbwiki.com) looks and feels very different from Wikispaces, and offers a few different features from Wikispaces. WetPaint (http://wetpaint.com) also looks and feels very different from both Wikispaces and PBWiki, but of the three it offers the widest array of site design options for customization. While both Wikispaces and PBWiki allow for free educational wikis that are ad-free, WetPaint does require a paid subscription to remove the Google Ads from the wiki pages. However, all three services offer many of the same basic features, and Wikispaces and PBWiki offer more enterprise-wiki features with a paid subscription.

The basic features available on Wikispaces, PBWiki, and WetPaint include:

- easy to use collaborative page/article creation and editing
- complete history of revisions and ability to restore pages
- use of widget for media embedding
- full content search
- RSS feeds
- document management and file sharing through image and file uploads
- discussion or talk pages
- wiki backups
- usage statistics
- use of tags for identifying key content of each page or article
- security access controls
- customization features: CSS, URL, page layout and design (limited with free versions)

MediaWiki (http://www.mediawiki.org) is the open-source software upon which Wikipedia is built, and therefore, MediaWiki will look and feel very familiar to anyone who has used Wikipedia — especially to anyone who has edited a Wikipedia article. I do not recommend MediaWiki to anyone who is just starting out, and who is only interested in exploring the content creation aspect of wiki use. MediaWiki installation and use is much more technical than the free wiki farm options but it does offer much more functionality than the free wikis.

The information in the preceding paragraphs is current as of the publication of this book. For updated information on the services, features, and subscription requirements of the wiki-hosting sites, you should visit each host's website for more information.

BASICS - The Anatomy of a Wiki

Article or Content Page

The article or content page is the page users see when they first visit the wiki or any of the pages of the wiki. This contains the content that is collaboratively created by the users. If users have editing rights, the article or content page can be edited by clicking on the "edit this page" button. Options for managing the page include editing, viewing revisions history, and discussing the content of the page with other users. These options are usually listed in tabs at the top of the page, however, some wikis such as PBWiki and WetPaint locate these options elsewhere on the page.

The process of adding content or editing content on a page is usually done with a basic visual editor much like the editing tools used in Microsoft Word. All wikis allow some markup language, but even novice users can add content or edit content without knowing the markup language. For more information on the markup language — or syntax — of the four wikis discussed in this book, please see the Appendix.

One word of caution: Wiki pages and articles cannot be edited synchronously. If two or more people are editing a wiki content page at the same time, some of those edits will be lost when both people attempt to save the edits.

Discussion Page

The Discussion page allows wiki users to communicate about the content of the page or article with which it is associated. You can think of this as a message board specifically for one article or one page. Each article or page has its own discussion or talk page. On the free wiki farm wikis, the discussion pages resemble traditional message boards on other websites, while on MediaWiki and other open-source packages the discussion page is simply just a blank page open for editing much like the article or content page. Wikispaces and MediaWiki both use the term "discussion" for this page and both place the link as a tab at the top of the page. PBWiki and WetPaint refer to this feature as "comments" and both locate the "comments" at the bottom of each wiki page.

On Wikispaces or MediaWiki, you go to the discussion page by clicking on the "discussion" tab at the top of your wiki page.

MediaWiki:

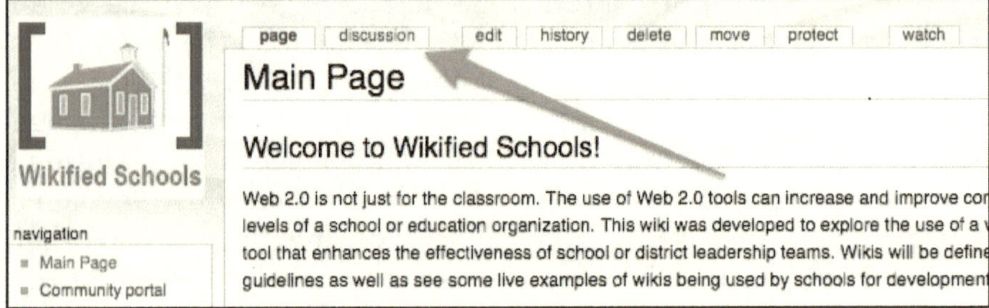

After clicking on the tab discussion, messages are posted using a basic WYSIWYG text editor:

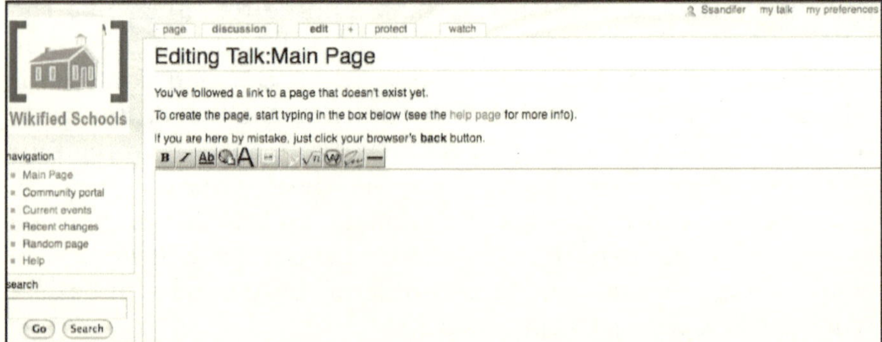

Wikispaces:

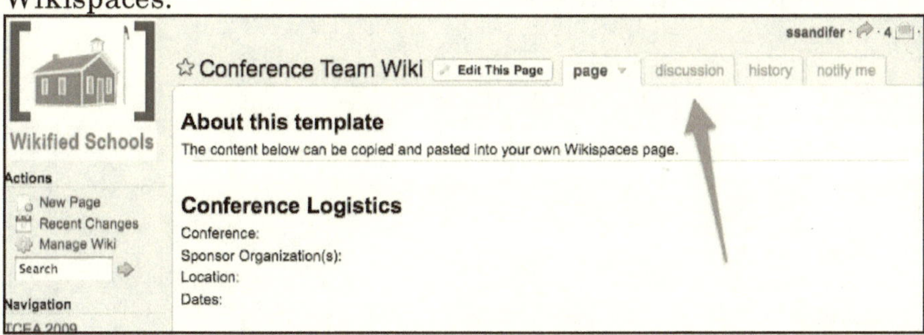

After clicking on the tab, discussion messages are posted using a standard form similar to those found on common message boards and web forums:

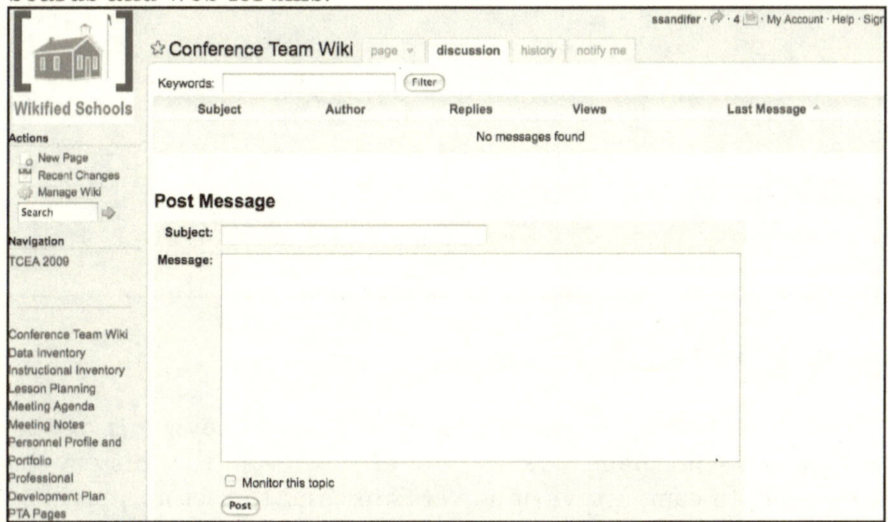

On PBWiki or WetPaint, you go to the comments section by scrolling down to the bottom of the page. There is no need to click on a tab, but users do have to be logged in to leave comments on the page.

Discussion on a PBWiki wiki:

Conference Team Wiki
PTA Pages
Comments (0)
Add a comment
Add comment
Printable version
pbwiki
Create your own educational wiki / Help
Terms of use / Privacy policy
About this wiki
Contact the owner / RSS feed / This wiki is public

Discussion on a WetPaint wiki:

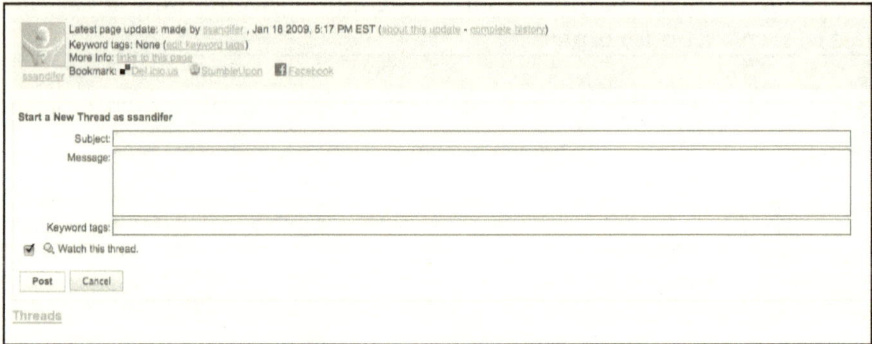

Revision History

The history tab contains all the saved revisions of the article or wiki page. Users are able to see the history of revisions, to compare various versions, and to restore previous edits by viewing this tab. Teachers find this feature helpful when tracking student participation on group projects, and all education users will find it helpful to not only be able to see what revisions were made, but to also be able to revert to previous revisions if a page or article becomes corrupted through the editing process.

Revisions on a Wikispaces wiki:

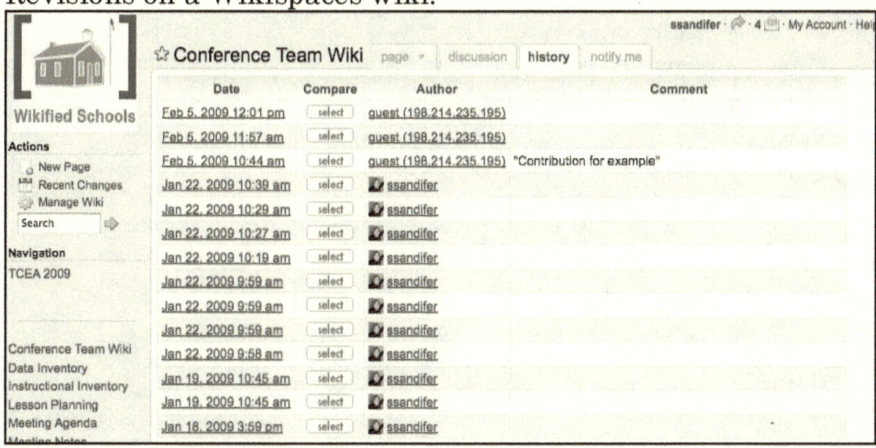

Revisions on a PBWiki wiki:

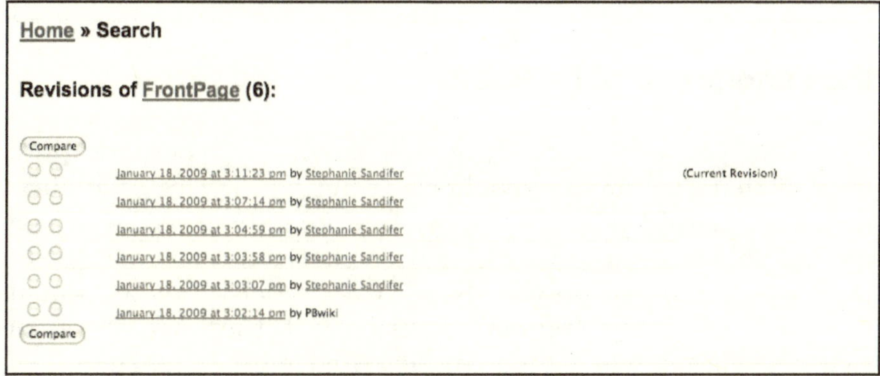

Revisions on a WetPaint wiki:

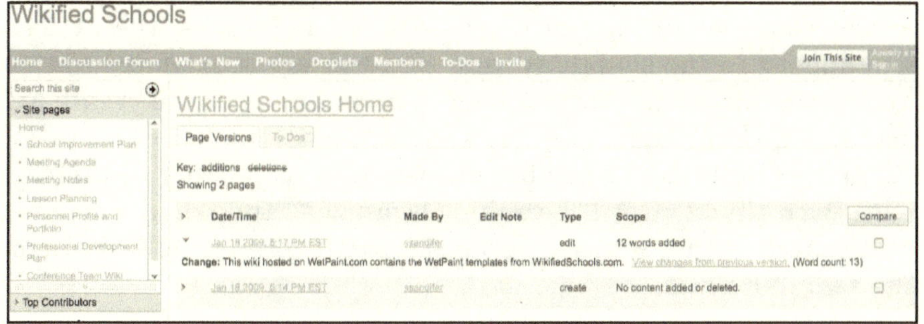

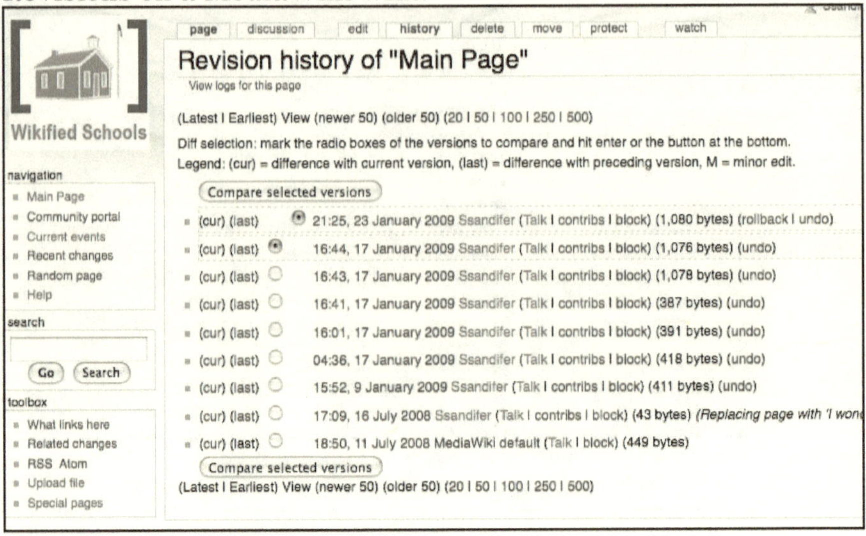

The importance of TAGGING

As you can probably guess, a wiki can become quite large if there are many people contributing articles and edits. Any large database or collection of documents is useless if we are not able to locate the information that is most important to us. As we discussed previously, all wiki articles can be located through the handy "search" function but they become even easier to locate when wiki authors and editors make use of "tags."

Each wiki article can be "tagged" with keywords. When a user searches on any of the associated keywords, the article will appear in the search even if the term is not included in the article title or content of the page. For example, if you create an article on the Venn Diagram that does not include the term "Graphic Organizer" anywhere in the text, you can still tag the page with the keyword "Graphic Organizer" and when someone else searches the wiki for "graphic organizers" it will show in the search results.

Adding tags on a Wikispaces wiki:

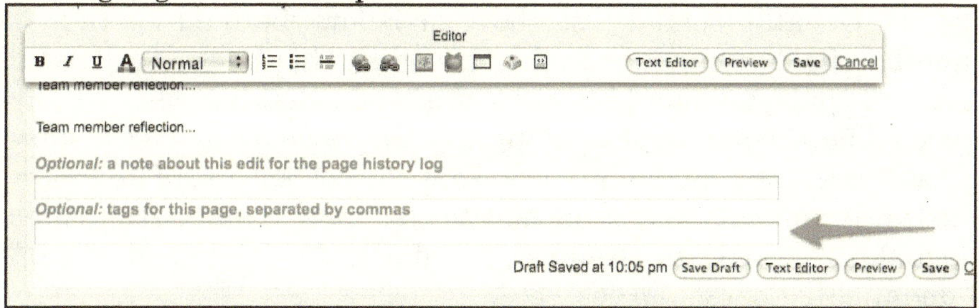

Adding tags on a PBWiki wiki:

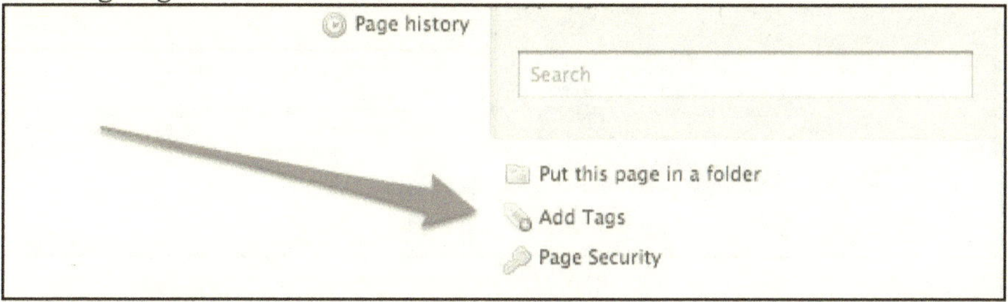

Adding tags on a WetPaint wiki:

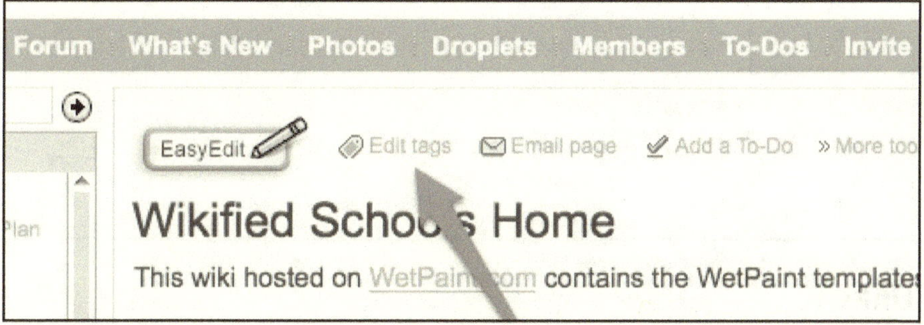

Wikispaces, PBWiki, and WetPaint all use the term "tags" for this feature. However, on MediaWiki this is referred to as "categories" and the process for generating the tags or categories is a bit different because MediaWiki does not provide a field in the editing process. Instead, MediaWiki users create "categories" by entering the following text anywhere into the body of the article or page (usually at or near the bottom): [[category:NameOfCategory]]

Edit or Page Notes

Usually located just above or below the field for tags is another field for entering editing notes. This is a very helpful feature that you should always use when making edits to any page. These notes appear alongside the revision on the history page, and they make it very easy for other users to know instantly the nature of your edit to the page. Examples of notes include: "edited to remove vandalism," "corrected typo," "updated list of employees," etc.

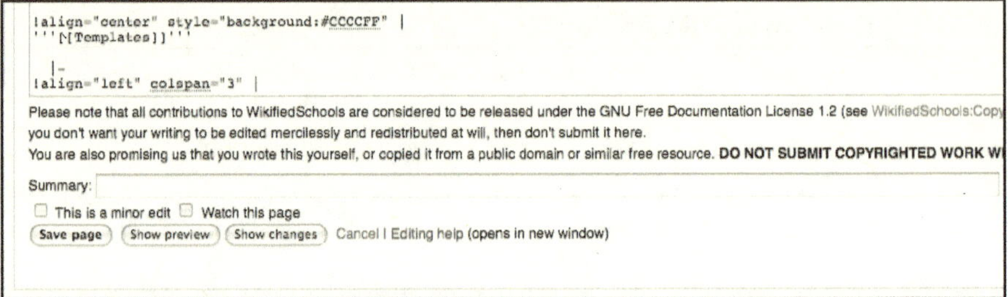

Notes on a Wikispaces wiki:

Links

All wiki pages allow editors to create a variety of links anywhere within the content of the page. The kinds of links that are possible include external links to any web page, email links to specific email addresses, links to uploaded content such as image files or documents, and internal links to other wiki pages. Internal links can even be created for pages that do not yet exist. After creating the link and saving the page, clicking on the link to the nonexistent page will trigger the creation of a new blank page that you can easily edit. This is a very handy feature when working on building content in your wiki.

Wiki-Etiquette

As with any form of collaboration or communication — in person or online — there are certain general guidelines that individuals must agree upon in order to communicate and collaborate effectively. While these guidelines or etiquette may differ from one culture to another, each is essential for maintaining a sense of order and productive communication. Here are just a few suggestions for community etiquette guidelines:

- Do not be rude or offensive when posting comments or making edits.
- Do not write "Click here for more information about Collaborative Learning." Instead, write "More info about Collaborative Learning." Avoid doing this for external links as well.
- Do correct typos or content errors.
- Do contribute original content or referenced materials. Follow normal citation and reference rules for academic writing to avoid plagiarizing or violating copyrights, and include links to original material if available online.
- Do use actual dates. For example, write "In August 2009 we implemented a new intervention program..." rather than writing "Last August we implemented a new intervention program..."
- Do add your signature to comments if applicable and do avoid using first-person references when creating wiki content.
- Do remain objective when adding or creating content. Pros and cons should be included when appropriate.
- Do be bold. Go ahead and create content or edit someone else's work. Remember that this is all about collaboration.
- Do not be offended if someone edits your work. Remember that this is all about collaboration.
- Do include "notes" when you make changes to explain what changes were made and why you made them.
- Do recognize useful content and give praise to constructive work that adds value to the wiki.

- Do help build structure. Allow for collaborative synthesis and structuring of the content by everyone.
- Do follow basic rules of grammar and avoid writing in ALL CAPS, which is considered "shouting" in online communications.
- Do use your own name and not an alias. This helps to build trust among the team and holds everyone accountable for his or her contributions.

You may find it helpful to also review the community guidelines set forth by the Wikipedia community. These guidelines are located at http://en.wikipedia.org/wiki/Wiki_etiquette. However, keep in mind that Wikipedia is an open wiki and your etiquette guidelines will most likely be different if you do not have an open wiki.

Finally, always remember the "Golden Rule" of wikis and be sure to include this on your wiki and when you introduce your staff to the wiki:

> "If it isn't on the wiki, it is not because it doesn't belong on the wiki... It's because YOU haven't added it to the wiki!"

Reflection Questions

What are your next steps towards wiki adoption?
What resources do you currently have in place to achieve these next steps??
What resources do you need in order to be successful in your wiki adoption efforts?

Chapter 6: Google Docs, Spreadsheets, and Presentations

As I was writing this book, I frequently reflected on the fact that I heavily rely on the Google applications for much of my collaborative work with my colleagues in addition to the use of our wikis. Google Docs, Google Spreadsheets, and Google Presentations are wonderful complementary applications for wiki use, and in some cases they make the wiki much more functional for all users. Here are some of the ways that the combination of Google applications and wiki use enable education professionals to collaborate more effectively and efficiently.

Google Docs

One of the challenges with wiki collaboration is that two or more people cannot simultaneously edit wiki pages. While two people can be editing the page at the same time, when both people try to save their edits some of the edits are lost as one "save" overwrites the other "save." This is generally not an issue because in most cases wiki editing happens asynchronously. If any particular collaborative project requires synchronous or simultaneous editing of the same document, you may want to consider using Google Docs instead of your wiki. Google Docs is the online text editing application developed by Google. Documents created in Google Docs reside on the Google server, but can be downloaded into Microsoft Word, .rtf, or .PDF format.

Additionally, the content from the Google Docs document can easily be copied and pasted into the wiki after the editing is complete. Google Docs works in much the same way as a wiki page where only one document is created and is shared between all users, revisions are tracked, and the document is hosted online rather than residing on a hard drive or traveling around (in multiple versions) on the email server. The biggest difference is that multiple users CAN edit one Google Doc simultaneously with no loss of data or content.

Google Spreadsheets and Forms

Google Spreadsheets and Forms are incredibly valuable for collecting information from users, and like Google Docs, multiple users can edit them simultaneously. As with any Google app, Spreadsheets and Forms can easily be embedded into a wiki page allowing users to interact with the form or data without leaving the wiki page. Some examples include the use of forms for providing feedback, conducting short surveys, and capturing other information directly from users.

Google Presentations

Google Presentations is Google's version of PowerPoint. Presentations can be created and shared online with all the same benefits of Google Docs, Google Spreadsheets and Forms. Presentations can be edited synchronously or asynchronously by multiple contributors, viewed online by offsite users in either synchronous or asynchronous situations, embedded into wiki pages and other websites, and can be downloaded as Microsoft PowerPoint files.

Chapter 7: Wiki Continued — Edit This Chapter

This book is unfinished. You have explored a variety of uses for wikis in your school environment and seen some examples. The final chapter involves you, the reader, and it does not exist inside this book. The final chapter, a wiki that you can contribute to, is located online at http://wikifiedschools.com. I invite all readers to visit and join the wiki. In doing so, you can experience firsthand the power of a wiki for collaboration, and you can contribute more ideas for using wikis in your schools. Additionally, the wiki contains other resources such as templates and sample wiki pages in multiple formats for your use.

Appendix

PBWiki Syntax

Type	Syntax	What you see...
Internal Link	CamelCaseLink or [Link]	Link
External Link	[http://www.externallink.com]	http://externallink.com
Headlines	! Level 1 !! Level 2 !!! Level 3 !!!! Level 4 !!!!! Level 5 !!!!!! Level 6	**Level 1** **Level 2** **Level 3** **Level 4** **Level 5** **Level 6**
Bold Format	**bold**	**bold**
Italics Format	"italics"	*italics*
Underline Format	__underline__	underline
Monospace Format	<code>monospace</code>	`monospace`
Strikethrough Format	-strikethrough-	~~strikethrough~~
Superscript Format	super^{script}	super^{script}
Subscript Format	sub_{script}	sub$_{\text{script}}$
Images	[http://www.URL.com/image.jpg]	Image displayed
Aligning Text	<left>, <center>, <right>	WYSIWYG Left, Right, Center
Text Indentation	Indented block	WYSIWYG indentation
Bulleted Lists	* Bullet #1 * Bullet #2 ** SubBullet #1	• Bullet 1 • Bullet 2 · Subbullet 1
Numbered Lists	# Number #1 # Number #2	1. Number #1 2. Number #2
Definition Lists	<dl>	
Horizontal Rule	----	

Wikispaces Syntax

<table>
<tr><th>Type</th><th>Syntax</th><th>What you see...</th></tr>
<tr><td>Internal Link</td><td>[[pagename]] or
[[pagename | alias]] or
[[spacename:pagename]]</td><td>pagename or
alias</td></tr>
<tr><td>External Link</td><td>[[http://somewhere.else]] or
http://somewhere.else or
[[http://somewhere.else | text label]]</td><td>http://externallink.com
or
text label</td></tr>
<tr><td>Headlines</td><td>= Level 1 =
== Level 2 ==
=== Level 3 ===</td><td>Level 1
Level 2
Level 3</td></tr>
<tr><td>Bold Format</td><td>**bold**</td><td>bold</td></tr>
<tr><td>Italics Format</td><td>//italics//</td><td>italics</td></tr>
<tr><td>Underline Format</td><td>__underline__</td><td>underline</td></tr>
<tr><td>Monospace Format</td><td>{{monospace}}</td><td>monospace</td></tr>
<tr><td>Images</td><td>[[image:image.jpg]]</td><td>Image displayed</td></tr>
<tr><td>Aligning Text</td><td>Via editor tool</td><td>WYSIWYG
Left, Right, Center</td></tr>
<tr><td>Text Indentation</td><td>> indent</td><td>WYSIWYG indentation</td></tr>
<tr><td>Bulleted Lists</td><td>* Bullet 1
* Bullet 2
** Subbullet 1
* Bullet 3</td><td>• Bullet 1
• Bullet 2
o Subbullet 1
• Bullet 3</td></tr>
<tr><td>Numbered Lists</td><td># Number #1
Number #2</td><td>1. Number #1
2. Number #2</td></tr>
<tr><td>Horizontal Rule</td><td>----</td><td></td></tr>
<tr><td>File Link</td><td>[[file:name.txt]]</td><td></td></tr>
<tr><td>Tables</td><td>|| table cell || table cell || table cell ||</td><td></td></tr>
<tr><td>Table of Contents</td><td>[[toc]] or [[toc | flat]]</td><td></td></tr>
</table>

WetPaint Syntax

WetPaint sites are edited with an editing toolbar that is completely WYSIWYG. All of the options on the toolbar are common to most word processing applications which makes them familiar to most wiki contributors.

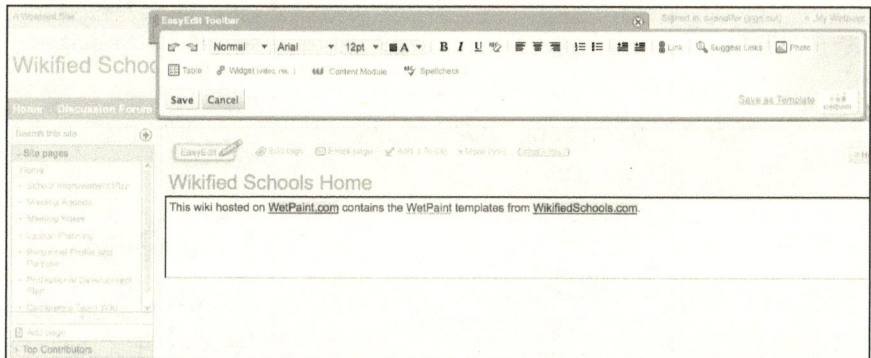

MediaWiki Syntax

<table>
<tr><th>Type</th><th>Syntax</th><th>What you see...</th></tr>
<tr><td>Internal Link</td><td>[[pagename]] or
[[pagename | alias]] or
[[spacename:pagename]]</td><td>pagename or
alias</td></tr>
<tr><td>External Link</td><td>[[http://somewhere.else]] or
http://somewhere.else or
[[http://somewhere.else | text label]]</td><td>http://externallink.com
or
text label</td></tr>
<tr><td>Headlines</td><td>==level 1==
===level 2===
====level 3====
=====level 4=====</td><td>Level 1
Level 2
Level 3
Level 4</td></tr>
<tr><td>Bold Format</td><td>'''bold'''</td><td>bold</td></tr>
<tr><td>Italics Format</td><td>''italic''</td><td>italics</td></tr>
<tr><td>Underline Format</td><td>__underline__</td><td>underline</td></tr>
<tr><td>Escape wiki markup</td><td><nowiki>no ''markup''</nowiki></td><td>no ''markup''</td></tr>
<tr><td>Images</td><td>[[image:image.jpg]]</td><td>Image displayed</td></tr>
<tr><td>Aligning Text</td><td>Via editor tool</td><td>WYSIWYG
Left, Right, Center</td></tr>
<tr><td>Text Indentation</td><td>:Indent text</td><td>indentation</td></tr>
<tr><td>Bulleted Lists</td><td>* Bullet 1
* Bullet 2
** Subbullet 1
* Bullet 3</td><td>• Bullet 1
• Bullet 2
o Subbullet 1
• Bullet 3</td></tr>
<tr><td>Numbered Lists</td><td># Number #1
Number #2</td><td>1. Number #1
2. Number #2</td></tr>
<tr><td>Definition Lists</td><td>;Definition
:item 1
:item 2</td><td>Definition
item 1</td></tr>
</table>

		item 2
Horizontal Rule	----	
File Link	[[file:name.txt]]	name.txt
Tables	|| table cell || table cell || table cell ||	
Table of Contents	[[toc]] or [[toc|flat]]	

Notes:

- Use of a heading created by single equal signs is discouraged as it appears with the same formatting and size as the page title, which can be confusing.
- An article with four or more headings will automatically create a table of contents.
- MediaWiki ignores normal line breaks. To start a new paragraph, leave an empty line. You can also start a new line with the HTML tags <br> or <br/>.

Wiki Adoption Action Plan

Wiki Adoption Action Plan (available on the wiki: http://wikifiedschools.com)
S.M.A.R.T. Goal:
Strategies:
Resources Needed:
Persons Responsible:
Timeline:
Evaluation:

S.M.A.R.T. Goals: Strategic, Measurable, Aligned, Results-oriented, Time bound

Glossary

Blog
Originally short for "weblog," a blog is just a web page that contains entries in reverse chronological order, with the most recent entry on top.

Blogroll
A list of recommended sites that appears in the sidebar of a blog. These sites are typically sites that are either on similar topics, sites that the blogger reads regularly, or sites that belong to the blogger's friends or colleagues.

Crowdsourcing
The process of tapping into the collective intelligence of a large group of people - usually volunteers - in order to complete tasks or projects. We see examples of crowdsourcing in Wikipedia.com where users voluntarily contribute to articles and on Digg.com where readers contribute, read, and rate news articles (the highest rated rise to the top of the news feed).

Podcast
An audio blog which is typically updated weekly or daily. Podcasts are recorded in mp3 format and may be downloaded to an iPod, or users may listen to podcasts on a desktop computer and other mp3 players.

RSS
Real Simple Syndication. A format for storing online information in a way that makes that information readable by many different kinds of software. Many blogs and web sites feature RSS feeds: a constantly updated version of the site's latest content, in a form that can be read by a newsreader or RSS aggregator.

RSS Aggregator
A newsreader gathers the news from multiple blogs or news sites via RSS, allowing readers to access all their news from a single web site or program. Online newsreaders (like Bloglines or Google Reader) are web sites that let you read RSS feeds

from within your web browser. Desktop newsreaders download the news to your computer, and let you read your news inside a dedicated software program.

Social book marking
The collaborative equivalent of storing favorites or bookmarks within a web browser, social book marking services (like del.icio.us or Diigo) let people store their favorite web sites online. Social book marking services also let people share their favorite web sites with other people, making them a excellent way to discover new sites or colleagues who share your interests.

Social networking
Social networking sites help people discover new friends or colleagues by illuminating shared interests, related skills, or a common geographic location. Leading examples include Ning, Facebook, LinkedIn, and MySpace.

Tags
Keywords that describe the content of a web site, bookmark, photo or blog post. You can assign multiple tags to the same online resource, and different people can assign different tags to the same resource.

Wiki
A wiki is software that allows users to easily create, edit, and link pages together. Wikis are often used to create collaborative websites and to power community websites. Wikis are used in many businesses to provide affordable and effective Intranets and for Knowledge Management.

Wiki farm
A wiki-hosting website that allows users to create their own wiki without installing software on their own server. These are excellent options for individuals and for exploring wiki use before committing to a larger wiki installation and implementation project. The most popular wiki farms include Wikispaces (http://wikispaces.com), PBWiki (http://pbwiki.com), and WetPaint (http://wetpaint.com).

Recommended Reading & Resources

Books:

Wikinomics: How Mass Collaboration Changes Everything by Don Tapscott and Anthony D. Williams

Wikipatterns by Stewart Mader

Using Wiki in Education by Stewart Mader

Here Comes Everybody: The Power of Organizing Without Organizations by Clay Shirky

Disrupting Class: How Disruptive Innovation Will Change the Way the World Learns by Clayton Christensen, Curtis W. Johnson, and Michael B. Horn

The Wiki Way: Quick Collaboration on the Web by Bo Leuf and Ward Cunningham

Mobilizing Generation 2.0: A Practical Guide to Using Web 2.0 by Ben Rigby

Blog Posts:

"Your job is to make something happen" by Scott McLeod
http://www.dangerouslyirrelevant.org/2008/04/make-something.html

"First Steps Toward Becoming a 21st-Century Educator" by Kim Cofino
http://mscofino.edublogs.org/2008/04/02/the-21st-century-educator/

"The Barriers May Not be so Great" by David Warlick
http://davidwarlick.com/2cents/page/3

"Disruption or Demand to Learn" by David Warlick
http://davidwarlick.com/2cents/index.php?s=disruption

"Purposeful Networking" by Kate Olsen and Stephanie Sandifer
http://www.katesays.org/2008/03/28/purposeful-networking/

"I'm on a Path — Come Join Me!" by Melanie Holtsman
http://onceuponateacher.blogspot.com/2008/02/im-on-path-come-join-me.html

"Don Tapscott Speaks Out on Education" by Vicki Davis
http://coolcatteacher.blogspot.com/2008/04/don-tapscott-speaks-out-on-education.html — Keynote for Horizon Project 2008

"9 Principles for Implementation: The Big Shift" by Sheryl Nussbaum-Beach
http://21stcenturylearning.typepad.com/blog/2008/03/10-principles-f.html

"ISTE's Refreshed Technology Standards for Students"
http://www.iste.org/Content/NavigationMenu/NETS/ForStudents/2007Standards/NETS_for_Students_2007.htm

Wikis & Other Websites:

http://www.classroom20wiki.com/Wikis
Provides an overview of wikis in education as well as links to many helpful resources and examples.

http://docs.google.com
Create your free Google Docs account and begin collaborating on documents, spreadsheets, and presentations. An excellent complement to your school or district wiki.

http://coollessons.wikispaces.com/Web-based_Communication
Wiki created for a course for educators interested in the use of Web 2.0 tools of blogs and wikis in classrooms. Many helpful resources included.

http://www.wikiindex.org/index.php?title=Welcome
WikiIndex lists over 3,400 different wikis, along with language, topics and wiki engine.

http://www.wikipedia.org/wiki/List_of_wikis
Wikipedia's List of Wikis

http://www.wikimatrix.org
Wikimatrix provides interactive comparisons of wiki packages.

http://www.springnote.com/en
Springnote is a free wiki-based online notebook, used for a wide variety of purposes - from writing notes, organization, scheduling, and group projects, among many other possible scenarios.

Wiki Farms (hosting) & Wiki Software:

Wiki Farms - Hosting Sites

http://atwiki.com/
@wiki – A completely free wiki service that offers WYSIWIG editing and password protected posts.

http://www.editthis.info/wiki/Main_Page
EditThis.info – Allows you a free 25 MB MediaWiki install with unlimited users and pages.

http://www.etouch.net/products/collaboration/index.html
eTouch SamePage – Allows teams to work in a collaborative environment on projects, free version allows for up to 5 users, 3 projects and 15 pages.

http://sites.google.com
Google Sites – Free website hosting and development application that works well for wiki creation.

http://www.littlewiki.com/wiki/
LittleWiki – Create a public or private free wiki with WYSIWIG or plain text editors.

http://pbwiki.com/
PBWiki – Offers free wikis, but they only have 10 MB of space. Paid solutions start at $99.50 a year. The service offers password-protected wikis for private or corporate situations.

http://www.wetpaint.com/
Wetpaint – A free wiki farm that focuses on bringing together the wiki format with blogs and forums. Very much directed towards fan-style sites.

http://www.wiki-site.com/index.php/Main_Page
Wiki-Site – Free MediaWiki accounts for individuals and groups, paid accounts get unique domains, access to stats and no advertisements, amongst other perks.

http://www.wikidot.com/
Wikidot – 300 MB free Wiki for whatever you want.

http://www.wikispaces.com/
Wikispaces – Starts at free 2 GB site for friends and families up to paid white label solutions.

http://www.xwiki.org/xwiki/bin/view/Main/WebHome

XWiki – Offers free solutions as well as paid options for enterprise users. Allows for application development and embedding in pages, along with RSS feeds to keep teams up on changes.

Stand Alone Wiki Software

http://sourceforge.net/projects/corendalwiki/
Corendal Wiki – A free and open source wiki package directed at corporate users. It's been a while since it has had any updates.

http://wiki.splitbrain.org/wiki:dokuwiki
DokuWiki – Aimed at small companies' documentation needs. Offers templating and plug-in support.

http://www.flexwiki.com/
FlexWiki – A free and open source wiki built on the .NET framework.

http://getwiki.net/-GetWiki
GetWiki – A modified version of MediaWiki that provides new features including XML importing.

http://www.ipbwiki.com/Ipb_Wiki:Integration_Of_Invision_Power_Board_with_MediaWiki
IpbWiki – A system that integrates MediaWiki with Invision Power Boards to make for a whole new wiki experience.

http://jamwiki.org/
JAMWiki – A Java based clone of MediaWiki that uses the same syntax for things such as footnotes, templates and more.

http://www.mediawiki.org/
MediaWiki – The same software that powers Wikipedia, MediaWiki is a PHP based, customizable system that is one of the most popular solutions due to its familiarity.

http://wiki.mindtouch.com/
Mindtouch – Free and open source wiki if you choose to run it on your own host, but if you prefer a managed solution for an

enterprise install, they offer various managed solutions.

http://moinmo.in/
MoinMoin – Has different built-in templates and allows for the support of documents. Popular framework being used by the likes of the GNOME and Ubuntu sites.

http://phpwiki.sourceforge.net/
PHPWiki – One of the oldest wiki solutions, first appearing in December 1999.

http://www.pmwiki.org/wiki/PmWiki/PmWiki
PmWiki – Built more for non-IT people and those that have no wiki background. Easy to change skins and appearance.

http://info.tikiwiki.org/tiki-index.php
TikiWiki – A content management system capable of handling many different jobs, but as the name implies, it favors wikis.

http://wikkawiki.org/HomePage
Wikka Wiki – Forked from Wakka Wiki, Wikka has some new features such as support for mind mapping.

Bibliography

Barrett, D. J. (2009). *MediaWiki.* Sebastopol, CA: O'Reilly Media, Inc.

Black, J. S., & Gregersen, H. (2002). *Leading strategic change: Breaking through the brain barrier.* New York: Prentice Hall.

DuFour, R., & Eaker, R. (1998). *Professional learning communities at work: Best practices for enhancing student achievement.* Bloomington, IN: Solution Tree.

Eaker, R., DuFour, R., & Burnette, R. (2002). *Getting started: Reculturing schools to become professional learning communities.* Bloomington, IN: National Education Service.

Higdon, J. (11/15/2005). Teaching, learning, and other uses for wikis in academia. *Campus Technology,* Retrieved 4/10/2008, from http://campustechnology.com/articles/40629/

Houston Independent School District retrieved on 2009-1-12 from http://www.houstonisd.org/literacyleadstheway

Howe, J. (2006). The rise of crowdsourcing. *Wired.* June 2006. Retrieved on 2009-1-6 from http://www.wired.com/wired/archive/14.06/crowds.html

Irvin, J. (2007). *Taking action on adolescent literacy: An implementation guide for school leaders.* Alexandria, VA: Association for Supervision and Curriculum

Development.

Lamb, B. (2004). Wide open spaces: Wikis ready or not. *Educause* Review. 39, 36-48.

Likert, R. (1967). *The Human Organization.* New York: McGraw-Hill.

Lunenburg, F. C., & Ornstein, A. C. (2004). *Educational administration: Concepts and practices.* Belmont, CA: Thompson/Wadsworth Learning.

Mader, S. (2008). *Wikipatterns: A practical guide to improving productivity and collaboration in your organization.* Indianapolis, IN: Wiley Publishing, Inc.

McGregor, D. (1960). *The Human side of Enterprise.* New York: McGraw-Hill.

The United States National Institute for Literacy retrieved from http://novel.nifl.gov/nifl/faqs.html

Reeves, D. (2006). *The learning leader: How to focus school improvement for better results.* Alexandria, VA: Association for Supervision and Curriculum Development.

Richardson, W. (2008). Footprints in the digital age. *Educational Leadership,* November 2008, 16-19.

Senge, P., Cambron-McCabe, N. Lucas, T., Smith, B., Dutton, J. and Kleiner, A. (2000) *Schools That Learn. A Fifth Discipline Fieldbook for Educators, Parents, and Everyone Who Cares About Education.* New York: Doubleday/Currency

Shelley, J. O. (1998). Factors that affect the adoption and use of electronic mail by K-12 foreign language educators. *Computers in Human Behavior,* v14 n2, May 1998, p269-85.

Shirky, C. (2008). *Here comes everybody: The power of organizing without organizations.* New York, NY: The Penguin Press.

Strauss, W., & Howe, N. (1997). *The Fourth Turning.* New York, NY: Broadway.

Tapscott, D., & Williams, A. D. (2006). *Wikinomics: How mass collaboration changes everything.* New York, NY: The Penguin Group.

Tapscott, D., & Williams, A. D. (2007). The wiki workplace. *BusinessWeek Special Report,* March 27, 2007,

Retrieved April 13, 2008, from http://www.businessweek.com/innovate/content/mar2007/id20070326_237620.htm?chan=search.

Toppo, G. (2009). Literacy Study: 1 in 7 U.S. adults are unable to read this story. *USA Today*, January 8, 2009. Retrieved January 29, 2009, from http://www.usatoday.com/news/education/2009-01-08-adult-literacy_N.htm.

Venners, B. (2004). The simplest thing that could possible work: A conversation with Ward Cunningham, Part V. *Artima Developer*, January 19, 2004. Retrieved January 25, 2009, from http://www.artima.com/intv/simplest.html

Wagner, T., Kegan, R., & et al., (2006). *Change leadership: A practical guide to transforming our schools.* San Francisco, CA.: Jossey-Bass.

Index

About the Author

Stephanie Sandifer, author of the Change Agency blog and a Literacy Content Specialist in Houston, Texas, is an experienced educator whose background includes teaching high school and college-level courses in studio art, design, computer graphics, animation, and research methods. She has also provided instructional leadership at the campus and district levels as a School Improvement Facilitator, Dean of Instruction, Small Learning Community Coordinator, and Literacy Coach. Throughout her career in education she has constantly advocated for technology integration across the curriculum. She presents locally, regionally, and nationally on topics ranging from technology integration, Web 2.0, effective instructional strategies, school improvement, and effective data analysis.

Change Agency: http://ed421.com

Wikified Schools: http://wikifiedschools.com

www.ingramcontent.com/pod-product-compliance
Lightning Source LLC
LaVergne TN
LVHW091006080826
845145LV00003B/1150

9780578012346